*Backdoor
Blessings*

Backdoor
Blessings

CHERYL FORBES

Zondervan Publishing House
Grand Rapids, Michigan

BACKDOOR BLESSINGS
Copyright © 1989 by Cheryl Forbes

First edition

Broadmoor Books
are published by Zondervan Publishing House
1415 Lake Drive, S.E.
Grand Rapids, MI 49506

Library of Congress Cataloging-in-Publication Data

Forbes, Cheryl.
    Backdoor Blessings / by Cheryl Forbes.
        p. cm.
    ISBN 0-310-44361-X
    1. Providence and government of God. 2. Blessing and cursing. 3.
Christian life—1960– . I. Title.
    BT135.F67 1989   88-34041
    242—dc19   CIP

Printed in the United States of America

89 90 91 92 93 94 / PP / 10 9 8 7 6 5 4 3 2 1

To those who find themselves
on the wrong side
of the backdoor

Contents

Going to Church

This book is about backdoor blessings—those things that usually are less than death but greater than a car that won't start—blessings in disguise because they come from God dressed in clothes we don't recognize. Although such blessings aren't easy or comforting, at least not on the surface, God uses them to break through our barrier of easy Christianity, for he wants to consume us. We want God at arm's length; he wants us in his arms. I'm not certain he prefers to use such methods, though I am sure that he must, because there are times when we make it impossible for him to hold us any other way. Let me tell you a story that may show you what I mean. It's a confession that I must make, one that you, also, may need to make.

*   *   *

Sunday after Sunday I dutifully get up, shower, dress, and leave for church; I've had the habit of attending church since I was too small to walk. Sometimes it's no more than that—a habit, and a habit I wish weren't quite so strong. I suspect that's true for more of us than would care to admit it.

But there are times when attending church is more than a Pavlovian response. I enter church, settle myself in my seat, read the bulletin, look over the congregation, nodding to the people and students I know, smiling vaguely at those I don't, and wait for the minister to mount the podium, raise his hands, and begin the opening response. He invites us to participate in a worship of our God, which, if my desire for God overcomes my automatic responses, startles me to involvement.

Not that I necessarily enter the congregation startled or ready to worship; I'm not sure many of us do. But something happens, even in my somnolent state, that I am never prepared for, probably couldn't prepare for. The minister reaches me with an off-hand word or casual phrase, a word or phrase so unexpected, so electrifying that he catches me off-balance and keeps me there throughout the service. Gone is habit, gone is the automatic response, gone is what I expect to hear or see. Instead, I come face-to-face with God, who does not deal in habit, automatic response, or human expectations. I don't know how all this happens, nor do I often like it— yet God reaches me no other way. Then, I worship God; then, I know why God insists on the habit, even though I don't always see the point. If I didn't have a habit of attending church or Bible study or praying, where would I be? Where would any of us be? Would God ever reach us?

Last winter, when I was in one of my sinful half-hibernations, I experienced the slam of God, which I've been thinking about ever since, despite my desire to forget about it and continue my life as uninterrupted as before. There I sat, nodding and smiling and half-sleeping, when the minister began his opening prayer, just one more of the thousands of opening prayers I've—almost, sort of— heard in my life. But what a difference.

I'm used to people praying in vague, pious abstractions, the kinds of phrases that are easy to sleep through, phrases that give a comfortable spiritual sheen to the day. Not so this morning. The minister thanked God on my behalf for the enemies he sends my way, the people who give me a pain in the neck, the difficulties I have with my children, the fights I have with my husband, and for good measure, all those circumstances that irritate and frustrate me. I had lots of those, I admitted to myself, but I'd never thought about them as things to thank God for. Then he said, "Help us see these as your blessings to us, blessings that come by the backdoor, blessings that break through our blind spot." Great, I thought. Sounds more like anti-blessings to me. And yet—did he have a point? Did my whole notion of blessing need to change?—because, despite myself, I saw how right he was.

But old habits die hard—for which I am grateful—so I continued to get up on Sundays, shower, dress, and drive to church, though I did so now with not a little apprehension, with a What next? on my mind. This church disturbs me—even threatens me—so that I can no longer settle comfortably in my seat and sigh that for an hour I have nothing to think about, no responsibilities to fulfill, no problems to solve. I know at any moment I may be hit broadside and must keep my wits about me and my feints and fists ready to avoid the blow. And yet, that broadside hit, that unexpected arrival of God, is the reason I go to this church and not one that is easy and comfortable, where my preconceptions about God are reinforced. I have to be honest—I long for God and yet, as with David, as with Paul, as with St. Augustine, as with

Pascal, as with C. S. Lewis, as with Lewis's infamous character Eustace Scrubb (in *Voyage of the Dawn Treader*), how I tremble at his entrance.

Then it came again—that opening prayer—only this time I heard words that nearly made me gasp aloud. I peeked out of half-closed and half-reverent lids to see if anyone else was as startled as I. It didn't seem so. People wore their complacent piety as easily as their suits or sweaters. Even my husband looked suitably contented. Maybe, I thought, I didn't hear right. Or maybe this is like Pentecost and each of us hears something different, something in his own language. Even now I'm not certain that it actually happened, though I suppose I could ask the minister—if I weren't so afraid of the answer.

So what did he pray? He asked God to make us insecure, uncomfortable, displaced; he asked God to keep us off-balance. I wanted to shout No! Leave me out of this prayer. That's *not* the business of God. Everyone knows that God is supposed to make us feel secure, and everyone knows that it's a minister's business as well. Isn't that what the Christian life is all about? Sure it is, I silently argued with the minister and, I feared, with God.

Feared? Absolutely. I don't want anti-blessings; I don't want God to act any way but how I determine he ought. This business was getting out of hand; some long-held and cherished notions about God's role and mine were being thrown all topsy-turvy, and the Christian life began to sound more like a threat than a comfort—and after years of faith. What happened to the platitudes?

My mind continued to snort throughout the rest of the service. I saw the connection—I couldn't escape it— between blessings that looked more like curses and comfort that was downright uncomfortable. This stuff, I thought, is not for me—not in twentieth-century middle America, heartland of comfortable Christianity. It's not as if I live in Palestine, with the Romans breathing down my neck, the Pharisees watching every move, and Jesus preaching about the kingdom being like the behavior of an immoral man. No one takes all that at face value any more; I certainly don't. Why, I can't. It just doesn't work; Jesus needs some updating and revising.

Although I thought all these things and more, the harder I tried to argue the more certain I became that I was wrong and the minister was right. God doesn't work the way I want him to—why, I might even call him sneaky. And as for comfort—well, I guess there's comfort and then there's comfort, just as Jesus would say there's peace and then there's *my* peace, which doesn't look or feel anything like we expect. What would the minister call it? My suspicion is he would call it grace under the sovereignty of God, which may not look too pretty or too warm from the outside, but in the cold it's the only cloak the Lord will offer. The question is, Do I want to put it on?

I suppose the answer to that is also a question: What else can I do? What else can any of us do?

Farewell to the Garden

Imagine Eden. Milton tried; so did C. S. Lewis. The Bible tantalizes us with a vision—work that refreshes, sweat that tastes sweet, relationships that bear no scars. How long did it last, I wonder. A day? A week? A month? Longer? Whatever the answer, "not long enough" is surely part of it.

So try to imagine Eden. I do, for I wish to return. Is that the longing in all our hearts? Is that the wistfulness of happily-ever-after? Or the poignancy of the fairy tale when the least likely character—could it be us?—turns into the prince or the princess? Don't we want to walk through the wardrobe door into the land where magic reigns, animals talk, and the King is coming?

Let's walk through the door. Don't you see it, just over there, between the CD player and the Queen Anne wing chair? It's taking shape in the paneling, the faint outline becoming clearer as we move closer and cross the long corridor into the room, now walking behind the sofa; yes, that's right. I know you see it, for you're walking faster. Don't you wonder how you missed the door all these years? Well, never mind that now. No, I know there's no doorknob; a slight push will move the door away from us and into the garden. What about the wall? There is no wall. Push and you will see; don't worry, I'm right behind you.

Smell the air. Wait—wait for me. Too late; you've run ahead and I may never catch up. What a lively step. You fairly float along the grass, soft as moss. Look at these trees. The sight goes straight to my stomach, feeding me with such luscious, yet strange, food that my senses seem all mixed up: sights I can taste, sounds I can smell. I won't worry, though it makes me a little giddy, because I'll surely become accustomed to the sensations. While you run ahead, I'll sit under this tree and smell the pool next to it. Now that I'm here I don't want to move, at least not right away. I'll leave exploring for later.

So this is what Eve relinquished for power; Adam too, of course; yet there's no denying Eve took the first step. Although I find it difficult to understand such a choice, now that I'm here, would I have done any better? No. Probably worse. That lust for control is so strong in me. If Eve and Adam thought, as they probably did, that they would rule all this, that might explain their choice.

But didn't they rule it anyway? Not exactly. A steward is not the same as a king; given a choice most of us would rather be king. Maybe that's why we refuse our stewardship back there—that other place where we came from, it seems so long ago. It's all a patch here, a brush stroke there, a little paint and plaster to hide the cracks, and a few blasts of deodorizer to disguise the odor. What a task to be stewards of that place when there are more people bent on cracking than plastering. Here the job would hardly *be* a job.

I don't know. It's probably a good thing we lost the door to this place, given our bent nature. Who knows what it would look like now—probably Brooklyn or the Bronx. But who could leave this place? Only kicking and screaming. Or begging for another chance. I can just hear them. "We'll be good, we promise; we won't do it again. We'll never disobey any more, if you just give us one more chance. It's not *fair*, not fair at all, to be kicked out of our home, the only one we've ever known, the one we've worked for and slaved for, just for one little mistake. What kind of king are you anyway?"

Or maybe they were too ashamed, the guilt too fresh, for them to talk that way, though it didn't take their progeny long to learn the vocabulary. Didn't Cain come up with something quite like it? But that's another story. I don't like thinking about the first story, sitting here in such splendor, because what Adam and Eve did affected me too. So typical, that behavior, never thinking about anyone but themselves, never thinking about *me* and what problems they caused me; well, that's long past, and I'm stuck with it, just as you are. I would have expected the lust for power to weaken over the generations, but it does seem that it grows stronger, doesn't it?

It's all part of the curse; isn't that what the King called it? Sometimes, though, I'm confused about that, because a curse causes withering and death and only that, which is not quite what we have. It seems to me that embedded in the toil and sweat and labor we have a deep blessing, what Milton and others have called the fortunate fall. Although I'm not willing to go that far, just looking around me, though, I see a little of their point. The King intended the Incarnation, which seems to me a striking example of a blessing, probably the archetype of blessings: the certain joy of life inextricably woven into the anger of death. We could have done worse, much worse. So the curse brought about the blessing, undoubtedly what people mean when they talk about the fortunate fall. Yet what about the problems along the way? Aren't those curses right enough?

The litany of brokenness, that's what it becomes: murder, jealousy, fear, spite, hatred, theft, anger, infidelity, disloyalty; not a blessing among them, nor among disease, infection, mental infirmities. Looking at it from this perspective, misery and nothing but resulted from Adam and Eve. But maybe there is another way to look at all this, that old wives' proverb of making the best of a bad situation—the King making the best of it, that is, or helping us do so; I doubt we could do it on our own. Look at Jacob and Esau, David and Bathsheba, or Samson and Delilah. Then there's Peter. Somehow, during the deep extremities of their curse the blessing came, perhaps because of the ultimate blessing the King embedded into the curse of Eve and Adam. Fortunate for us, there's no escaping the principle that we are blessed while we experience a curse.

Oh, you're back, are you, and not even breathing hard. Yes, I'm ready to explore a little, though first I'd like to taste the sight of that pool on my tongue. I'm a little parched—too much talking to myself, I guess. No, I'm not going to hurry; why should I? We have plenty of time, if that word holds any meaning here. I know that we'll need to return to that other place, though I can't see the door, can you? When we do, it will be time to go. But first— what was it you wanted to show me?

Friends and Enemies

I walked into the office, shy and scared and longing for this job, my dream job since I had been fourteen. Something in me said I would be hired. So what if it was just a secretarial position? At least it was a start. "If you get this job," I thought to myself, "in three years you'll be writing and editing." Then I laughed at myself and my phony confidence.

As I sat in the reception area waiting to be interviewed, I saw her walk by, a manuscript in hand. She walked not only as if she belonged there, but as if she couldn't belong anywhere else. But it wasn't just her walk that made me notice her. I had never seen anyone look more like Maria Callas, the prima donna of all prima donnas—haughty, aristocratic, fascinating, and repugnant simultaneously. Maybe sophisticated or worldly best sums it up. She seemed the City to me; I had barely left the classroom and the country. My brown and gold dress, which I had so carefully chosen, seemed ordinary, the fabric cheap, compared to the exotic, expensive outfit she wore. "Oh, boy," I thought to myself. "How will I ever fit in if *she's* any example of the editors?" Just then my future boss asked me to come into his office, and I got the job. Although I longed to ask, "Who is *she*?" I didn't dare.

It didn't take me long to learn who she was or that she didn't like me. Of course, I didn't like her either. Everything about her put me off—her austere appearance, her cold manner, her bookishly correct grammar. She's the only person I know who never says, "It's me," or confuses her nouns and pronouns. I soon learned why "hopefully, it won't rain" is incorrect; how foolish I was to dangle my modifiers; and the difference, for those interested in the niceties of language, which she was, between *that* and *which*. Although I was grateful someone had finally bothered to teach me what I should have learned in sixth grade, I still didn't like her.

Perhaps it was her resemblance to the great opera singer; perhaps it was the first sentence she ever spoke to me—an icy response to a naïve question. As she was leaving for lunch on a cold January day, I noticed that she carried a book of Beethoven sonatas. "Oh, do you play the piano?" I asked—but something in the words, something in my tone, or just *something*, didn't sit right with her. "I ought to," she replied with a decided sniff in her voice. "I've been studying for twenty years." I recall gulping an inarticulate "oh" before I returned to my desk for my bag lunch. I'd never known anyone who had studied the piano that long; my seven years at the keyboard seemed so insignificant, though no one I knew—until her—had studied longer. I didn't speak to her again for some time; I didn't want to risk another snubbing.

Of course, I was the newest and lowliest member of the staff—a mere secretary. So what if I had a degree in English? So did she. So what if I read? So did she. So what if I sang? She hated singers, a characteristic of many instrumentalists who don't consider singers musicians. I had ambitions—to write, to edit. She chose not to write and already was an editor, *the* copy editor, under whose pencil every news story, article, book review, or editorial fell. What readers knew of the magazine—its style, its structure, its linguistic precision—came from her and from no one else. It didn't take me long to understand who had the last say. On the other hand, I had no say at all.

No, I didn't like her, and I didn't think I ever would. Although I wanted to work my way out of typing for someone else and into typing for myself, I knew she would stand in my way, because she would judge, and judge harshly, every word I wrote. What an advocate she could have been, and yet what a barrier she was to my ambitions. I tried not to show how much I disliked her, everything about her, including the respect she had among the rest of the staff—but I'm sure she knew it. What I couldn't figure out, though I thought about it often, almost obsessively those first few hard years, was why she had disliked me on sight. Over and over I asked myself, "What did I do?" I still have no answer.

Each of us has people we can't like no matter what they or we do; I suppose I fell into that category for her. I know she did for me. But despite the antipathy we felt toward one another—or rather because of it—things began to change. Editors gave me writing assignments, which I eagerly completed, only to have her rewrite every word, which I would then retype as she had rewritten it. I begged for work, any work—research, proofreading, paste-up, and of course, more writing. Each assignment came back rewritten; she never quarreled with my ideas, just the way I expressed them. I tried to understand what I was doing wrong, how I could write more clearly and precisely. But I wasn't making any progress. Then, for an anniversary of Tolstoy, either his birth or death, I can't remember which, I wrote a simple editorial—and it came back from her office just as I had sent it. What a triumph. I'd finally figured out what to do.

But I soon decided the editorial was a fluke, a mistake, because she went back to rewriting my stuff just as she had been. Hadn't I learned anything?

Finally, I asked her for a book I could read on how to write, silently blasting those professors who had told me what a good writer I was. Her frigid reply, "I don't know of any," did not put me off. I insisted that there must be *something* I could study. Probably more to remove me from her office than from a desire to help someone she considered so obviously lacking in ability, she grudgingly said, "Well, there's Strunk and White, *The Elements of Style*." I wrote the information on a slip of paper and immediately put it on my Christmas list, and my mother dutifully bought the book, wrapped it, and placed it under the tree. I read it and read it and read it again—and still Carol continued to rewrite my copy.

My mother says I'm stubborn—and she's probably right. Given encouragement I continue on much as before, but given resistance I work fiendishly. Carol's resistance made me determined to conquer the art of clear expository writing, made me determined to conquer myself, and made me determined to conquer her. If she had been as complimentary as my college professors, I would have learned nothing. If she had liked me, I would have learned nothing. If I had liked her, I would have learned nothing. Somehow, for whatever reason, I needed that adversary relationship, needed her to force me to think and think clearly, because that was the real problem: no one had ever taught me how to think. She did.

Could I learn from an enemy? Someone I considered a pain in the neck? Absolutely. And slowly, over a few years, we became friends, something I never thought possible that snowy January day.

Because it happened so slowly, I never recognized that a change had come about, though I recall a day when I knew that I no longer disliked her and that she no longer disliked me. Then, another day, I recognized that my respect for her was genuine. Oh, we never became intimate friends, though we did entrust each other with some confidences. We exchanged dinner parties, and she never hesitated to tell me when she thought my behavior or conversation dull or monopolizing. When I wanted my future husband to meet my friends, I began with her, and she and her husband were near the top of our short wedding list.

My debt to Carol is great. As I check off what I know because of her, the conclusion is inescapable: She began my education. Even today, after almost twenty years, I seldom write anything without wondering what she would do to it or how she would judge it. I edit the way she edited; I even teach writing the way she taught me. "How else can someone learn to write but by being rewritten?" I ask my students.

And that, I suppose, is the greatest compliment I can give.

A Friend in Need

Janet had moved around the company for several years, caught in uncomfortable positions or programs that were on their way out. She had suffered with several bosses who let her do much of the work, only to take the credit when it was handed out. At last, she had a position she enjoyed, working for someone she respected, who didn't want her to do his job as well as her own. Then the unthinkable happened: The division head called her into his office to say that he was replacing her. She was one of ten people he fired that day. "Why?" she asked. "Why me?" Division heads don't like those questions.

Yet he provided some answers: poor profits, cuts in the work force mandated from above, ending a product line that left a manager without a job—and they are less expendable than administrative assistants. So the manager got Janet's job, and Janet got a month's severance, not much for a woman with two children to support and an ex-husband who refused to pay child support. "I'll be glad to give you a reference," the division head told her as he showed her the door. Was she supposed to feel grateful? Janet wondered.

She was not the first to feel the effects of the

company's difficulties; she would not be the last. Nor was she the first of my friends to be fired, either there or at other organizations. Years earlier I had experienced the painful firing of a close friend—his family was a second family to me. It happened the Friday before Christmas, a time only an utterly insensitive manager would choose, for nothing is more dehumanizing and destructive than losing a job, any job.

"What will you do?" I asked Janet when I called her. "I don't know; I don't even know where to begin looking for a job." She and I both knew the big employers in the area, and we also knew how difficult jobs were to find. But more difficult than losing a job she loved was the prospect of leaving the people who were more than her co-workers; they were friends, they were family. "I feel as if I'm going through my divorce all over again," she said—and I knew what she meant. Losing a job is just like a divorce.

Although we talked for some time, I knew I had no comfort to give. How would she tell her children that food might be hard to come by and that the shoes they needed would have to wait? How would she keep from resenting her ex-husband even more for contributing to her precarious financial situation? Again she asked, "Why me?"

At least Janet didn't fall into the trap many people do—she didn't avoid looking for a job. She rewrote her resume immediately, filed with an employment agency, and began sending letters of inquiry to prospective employers. When she left her job in midsummer, she had hoped to find another before her severance pay ended; with each interview she gained confidence that all would be well. "We'll call you," she heard numerous times. "We'll probably bring you back for a second interview," people told her. Although she waited, the phone never rang; no second interviews came her way. Businesses today want people with college degrees, even for an administrative assistant, which she didn't have. Should she return to school? Should she try once more to get the child support her ex-husband owed? Should she move? Maybe she should look at her problem from a different angle, but how? By the end of summer she still wasn't working.

As she waited, her bitterness grew—bitterness toward her old employer and the division head who felt forced to fire her, toward her ex-husband, and worst of all, toward God. Although she had moments when she caught a glimpse of the grace of God, she had too many other times when all she saw was his desertion—another failure in a life suffering from too many failures. Pray? She could not.

Occasionally, she called during those bad times, but I had nothing to say—nothing, that is, that would make any difference. Instead, I asked her for lunch or to a party or to spend the afternoon drinking iced tea on the deck. Although we tried to talk of other things, the conversation returned time and again to finding a job.

Bill was the one bright spot, her support and encouragement. For several years they had been friends, and the rest of us waited to hear of their decision to marry. Of course, we believed that Bill was the solution to Janet's difficulty—as much as anyone could be. But did Bill? Did Janet herself? It was maddening to spend hours talking with her and never once hear her mention his name, maddening and unnatural. When my curiosity eventually overcame my manners, I asked.

Janet didn't say much, though she smiled, which

didn't satisfy me, so I blurted out, "We're all waiting for you to get married, you know. Well . . . ?" Even that didn't bring more than an "I don't know." I had to be content with her smile—and the information that she was going to California to meet his parents. At least that showed progress.

Little by little during her months without a job she became reconciled to her situation, and, maybe, a little to God. Her perspective began to change to see the glimmer of blessing imbedded in the hardship. What if she *had* found a new job immediately? Would she have been free to fly to California? And then, finally, she called with the news: she and Bill were getting married—in a month. "Why wait?" she asked, adding, "Boy, am I glad I don't have a job yet. I'd *never* get everything done if I had to work all day." Then she stopped, realizing what she had said. "I can't believe I'm saying that—but it's true."

Her suffering, though, had not ended. How could she know when she called me that doctors would discover cancer in her father only a few days before her wedding? Her time was divided between marriage plans and the hospital. She handled this with great equanimity, at least on the surface. Yet even more remarkable to me were the people she invited to her wedding—the division head who fired her, the person who replaced her. Forgiveness is the work of God, who completes his job every time.

Father and Sons

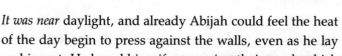

It was near daylight, and already Abijah could feel the heat of the day begin to press against the walls, even as he lay on his mat. He heard his wife preparing their meal, which he hoped would be cooling yoghurt and cucumbers. By now, he knew, his son had been out to attend the flocks and herds.

Such a faithful son, not like the other one. Abijah sighed. How could a father have deserved such a one as that other, yet so bright, so full of life. To have merged the two—that would have made a son of such perfection, such pleasure, the loyalty and steadfastness of the one with the lively air of the other. But not in this universe can a man have perfection, of that Abijah was sure. He sat up, ready for a drink of water, wondering for the thousandth time whether he would ever see his son again, repeating in his mind the harsh scene when the boy had left.

"Give it to me," Joath had shouted. "You know I don't fit in here—all work, all sweat and fields and smelly sheep. I'm for the city, not the country. This life's a nuisance, an annoyance. I need to be my own man, and I think it's time." Breathing hard, he glared at his father.

Abijah trembled with the audacity of his son. Never

had he heard of such a request, not in this village or any village. A son who wanted his inheritance before the father was dead?

"Son, you and your brother will have your inheritance once I'm gone." Abijah raised his hand and said, "I know, I know. That's what you want—my death. Better you should have killed me than brought this shame to my house and to the village. Stay by me, and let's work out our differences. Don't go now. If you leave, what will be left to you?"

"Father, whether you give me my inheritance or not, I'm going. I won't sleep in this place another night. You're too rigid, too self-righteous, too judgmental. Holiness, being clean, praying all day—those are the only things that count to you. Well, what if someone doesn't believe those things? As for this village, who cares for these people? They're no different from you. And it doesn't matter what they think of me, for I won't be back. Ever. I'll no longer eat their dust."

Abijah turned away from his son, wondering what to do. He was bound to leave, sooner or later, that was obvious. Not even the estate could hold him here much longer. But what would be best? To give him his inheritance and watch him liquidate a third of the estate, as he surely would, and at a loss, or refuse to help him destroy himself, which is what he'll do, his father thought to himself. There seemed to be no right answer. How did all this come about? Abijah paced the floor while Joath impatiently waited for an answer.

"Give me time to think—a few hours. After evening prayers, I promise you an answer," Abijah said to his son.

"No later," and Joath left the house, just as his mother entered it.

"You heard?" asked Abijah.

"I heard. You've pushed him too far. I told you and told you that the boy won't be pushed. Now we'll lose him."

"You told me—and I told you not to baby him. Always it's been Joath this and Joath that. Joath's too weak to help shear sheep or Joath's too smart to pick figs; let him study with the Rebbe. See now how smart your Joath is." This was an old, old argument, which Abijah, seeing his wife's face and feeling his own hurt, no longer had stomach for. "Well, no matter," he said, putting his arm around his wife's shoulder. "No doubt we both share the blame, though I don't know where we went wrong. He wasn't always so disobedient. Remember how he loved to follow me around the pastures? Remember how he sat in my lap when I told of the Exodus during the Seder? Our younger son. I've got to let him go."

"But the inheritance? What about the inheritance? He doesn't know how to use such a gift. And what will Joachim say to that? We can't lose both our boys."

"Joachim will understand. He may be a little self-righteous, but I'll talk to him. I'll divide the estate, and then Joachim will be in control; he'll enjoy that. Maybe better now than when I'm dead. As for Joath, he may waste it, but what's to prevent him doing that later anyway? No, wife, I've made my decision. We will mourn for him as for one dead, and then we will live as before. Joachim will marry and give us grandsons. What do you say to that?"

His wife had nothing to say; Abijah had made his decision.

It was late when Joath returned, smelling of strong drink. Without a word, his father handed him the papers he had drawn up. "Now I'll have it all," said Joath, visions of the voluptuous Rachel moving before him. Not saying thank you or good-bye, Joath grabbed the pack he had prepared earlier in the day and left. First money, then Rachel, he thought, and then on to a country where people really knew how to enjoy themselves.

The voice of Abijah's wife startled him. "Why are you sitting there staring, husband? Come, the meal's ready. Joachim and Sarah have eaten long since, and our neighbors are all up. I think her time is near, maybe today. Soon we'll have the grandson you promised me. Abijah, are you listening to me?"

"Yes. No. Yes, I'm listening, but I don't know for what. Near her time, you say? Is everything prepared? Yes, of course it is; why am I asking such a question? I'm getting feeble-minded." He no longer seemed to hunger for yoghurt. "How long have we waited?"

"Why, what do you mean? Joachim only married last year, and already we are to have a grandson. Of course, it took him long enough to agree to Sarah, but he seems pleased with her. She's made him a good home and herself a good daughter-in-law."

"No, not for Joachim, for Joath. How long have we waited for his return?"

"Joath is dead, old man, if that's what you've been moping about for these last few days. We've had no word of him in years. You said to mourn and forget. For a change, take your own advice."

"You're right, of course, and yet—"

"And yet nothing. We've got Sarah and Joachim and the new one to think about, so let's not—" Just then, Joachim rushed into the house.

"It's time, she says."

"So stay with your father, boy. It may be awhile, though Sarah's strong." Picking up the cloths she had washed and set aside, she left the house.

"Finish the chores?" Joachim nodded.

"Good thing. Hard to wait, though, isn't it?" Joachim nodded again.

"Well, since you don't seem up to talking, I guess I'll get on with my own work. Call when you hear." This time Joachim grunted.

It was nearly dusk when Abijah heard Joachim coming in his direction. "A boy and big," said his son. "Mother says Sarah had a hard time but that I can see her soon, once she's cleaned up. I'm off to let the Rebbe know. Sarah wants to call him Abrajim after her father, if you have no objections."

"Why should I?" Abijah turned away, sorrowing over another insult, another shame. Shouldn't the child have been named for him? But what did it matter to one long dead?

And so the days passed, the little one growing and Joachim prospering, though every now and again Abijah saw signs of his son's increasing arrogance and self-righteousness. As Abijah's comforts and desires were less and less considered, he wondered why his life had fallen out as it had. Other villagers, he knew, pitied him and secretly despised him for the cowardly manner in which he had dealt with his sons, though none would dare to have the bad manners to say so. They left him his face, if nothing else.

Then one morning, just as he was about to leave the village, he saw a traveler coming toward the town. Abijah knew, knew without a doubt, who the traveler was. How dare he return? wondered Abijah. Surely the boy knew what the villagers would do to him once they saw him. Secretly, they might despise Abijah, but publicly they would repay his shame and spit on Joath, throw stones and sticks at his returning son. Abijah had to reach the boy before the villagers to show them that the one they had buried and mourned was alive again. So he ran.

Not for years had he done anything so undignified, so out of keeping with his status as a great landowner of the village. He could almost hear his neighbors saying, "See, what do riches really buy in this life?" Well, he no longer cared. Although he stumbled a little, he continued to run until his breath had left him and he had reached his boy.

"What? What are you babbling?" Abijah asked his son, whose prepared speech was not going as planned. "A hired servant? No, how can this be, when you are my son. You must be all or nothing." Abijah put his protective arm around the boy and began returning to the village, this time in a slow, dignified step. "We have time, much time, to learn of your adventures."

But the boy could not stand silence. "I've wasted my inheritance. I've slept with whores and drunks. I've even slept with pigs and eaten what they have eaten. How can I return to the village any other way but as a hired servant?"

Abijah paused in his step. "My son, still you do not understand, though some day you will know this as a great blessing, just as I count these years. Don't be afraid of the villagers, either, for at our feast today they will greet you as one who was lost and is found, as one who was dead but now has returned to life. You will live here with your mother and me, and your brother will not turn you out."

By now, the village was alive with shouts as the people saw who entered. When Abijah's wife went out to see the commotion, Abijah said to her, "Bring me the first robe and the signet ring. Have the servant kill the calf. Today is a feast."

When she returned with the robe and ring, Abijah gave them to Joath. "Go and greet your friends," he said. "Now where is your brother?"

Joachim, just returning from the field, understood, and because his hatred for his brother boiled over in his heart, he refused to enter the village. "If father has no sense of shame, then I'll not worry about another small insult," Joachim thought to himself. But he knew that should Abijah order him to the feast he must go.

"Son, come to the feast. Be reconciled with your brother."

Joachim turned his face from his father, who tried again.

"You have the inheritance. Joath has had his and cannot receive more. What I have belongs to you. Show mercy, if not for my sake, then for your own."

"Go back to your guests, father, and let me think a little."

So Abijah returned. Did Joachim follow?

I Didn't Ask

I grew up in a family of six, large enough for conflict and too large for giving in—at least with our personalities. How we loved our own way and hated the thought of that mealy-mouthed word, *compromise*, especially when my sisters and I were teenagers. Compromise was for weaklings or pushovers.

It was bad enough to give in to my sisters, but it was unthinkable to give in to my parents, who didn't believe in compromise any more than I did. No matter what it was—clothes, school, hair, my attitude—my parents and I were at odds. If I wanted to go to a basketball game, I had to study. If I wanted to go to the pool, I had to iron. If I wanted to go for a walk, I had to baby-sit my brother.

To be fair, I had my share of fun despite the chores. My mother, who tried to create a joyous atmosphere, succeeded more often than she failed, because my friends, like Carolyn, loved to visit; yet teenagers rarely notice the good things because they concentrate so much on the bad.

We lurched from conflict to conflict, none of us wanting to give an inch. "Why can't I go out with Harvey Martin?" I cried. "He's too old for you—or you're too young," my mother answered. "You're ruining my life," I returned, and I believed it; my mother thought she was preserving my life.

When we fought, I made her life miserable. "Look at all the things I've done for you," she'd say, enumerating them. What did I care, when wild Harvey Martin was out and tame Jim Kennedy was in? I wanted her to give me what I wanted, my idea of compromise, not tell me all the sacrifices she made for my welfare. It seemed to me that she gave me what I didn't want and refused to give me what I did. To her litany my standard response was, "I didn't ask you for any of those things."

Of course, inside myself I knew that I had asked for a new dress or a special dinner or to borrow the car, if only indirectly. But I couldn't admit it when she refused to give in to yet another whim. How better to hurt her than to reject what she offered me?

"I didn't ask" negates every loving act. It says, "You're unimportant, incidental, a nuisance, bug off, leave me alone, don't do me any favors." I suppose it's all part of growing up and away from dependence on our parents, but some of us manage this more gracefully than I did.

Allen Jr.'s words brought all this back to me. "I didn't ask you for all these lessons," he said, accusing his father and me of trying to run his life. I recognized not only the words but the tone of voice—and I was as shocked as I'm sure my mother must have been when I said them. "You didn't ask?" I responded. "No, it was all your idea," he said. Our idea to give him four guitar lessons a week? I wondered to myself. I hadn't recalled anyone but Allen himself setting up his lessons; we had merely agreed to pay for them. But he had decided we were pushing him; suddenly "he hadn't asked." It must have been someone else who said to us, "Can I have a lesson tomorrow? How about the day after?" My mother had warned me that someday I would understand. When Allen spoke, I knew that day had arrived. How, I wondered, could he be so ungrateful? Although a relationship is not a one-way street with arrows marked in our direction, we don't want anyone, especially a parent, to remind us of this truth. Allen certainly didn't; nor had I when I had been his age. So it's "Get lost and leave me alone, not interested, you're unimportant to me."

Yet in many ways we say to God what I said to my mother and what Allen said to us, which is merely another way of saying, "Bless us our way; don't give us what we need but what we want." At the same time, we accept his gifts without acknowledging the giver, just as I accepted my mother's sacrifices and Allen Jr. accepted the money to pay for his lessons without a thank you. Nevertheless, despite our ingratitude and our lying words, God continues to care about us, just as my mother continued to care about me and we continue to care about Allen.

At times God's concern oppresses us; then he seems to disappear, as if to say, "Let's see how you really like it." Although we don't want to be left alone, we're also reluctant to accept God on his terms, which is, finally, the only choice he gives.

Never Failing

I don't fail—an axiom of my life. What I set out to do, I do, thanks in part to my mother's words to me as I grew up: "You can do anything you put your mind to." And I believed her—except when it came to math, though I didn't figure math counted, which was strange, since mother usually gave me the you-can-do-anything speech *about* my low math grades. Nevertheless, I firmly believed her in every other circumstance.

I set goals, big and small; I finished what I started; I worked hard. I've got those virtues embedded in my marrow, those northern European, Reformed virtues. With each job I took, I heard my mother say, "I never left a job that my boss didn't want me to stay." When I called to tell her of another promotion or another raise, she responded, "Well of course I knew you would get it." As far as my mother was concerned, I couldn't fail, despite my faults, which she never neglected to point out when she saw them. But smart she thought me, a hard worker she knew.

My father, too, was a never-failer. Hadn't he managed, without a high-school education, to become a well-paid, successful specialist in international logistics for the

Navy Department? Or take my grandpa, who had one of the best dairy farms in Wisconsin. Hadn't his farm been pictured in the paper because it was so special? Then there's grandma. She never had trouble with math; she even taught it. And she could speak several languages— German, Danish, Norwegian, and English. She also worked hard—and she never failed.

Sturdy, upright stock: that was my family. My sister, too, was a never-failer—a straight-A, Phi Beta Kappa character. Then came the day I stopped to see her on my way home from a graduate seminar. "You'll be over for dinner Saturday, won't you?" I asked. She started to wring her hands, which I'd never seen anyone do before; I thought it only happened in novels. "What's wrong?" I asked. "Harry and I are getting a divorce," she began, and before I could say a word she added, "How am I going to tell mother? People in our family don't *get* divorced." What she really meant, of course, was that people in our family don't fail.

These were my thoughts the day I sat in his dark office and heard the words "I'm restructuring the division and dispensing with your job." What a euphemism. I heard, "You're fired; you've failed," and I knew that's what my family would hear too. What could I say to him? That people in my family don't lose their jobs? That I'm a never-failer? That I finish what I start? In this case, someone else was finishing things for me.

Then I thought about money. I *had* to work to help meet our mortgage and other expenses. Nor could we move, because my husband had just signed a two-year teaching contract. I faced the end of my career, not my former boss. What would I do?

I didn't really listen to the rest: "It's not that you

haven't done a good job; don't worry about money; this is the best thing for you; why don't you write full time." What right had he to determine my future? Most of the time I wasn't too keen on God sticking his hand in my affairs; I certainly couldn't tolerate another person doing it. After he gave me a week or two to clear up my projects before my last day, I left his office thinking of the most irrelevant things. "Well, at least I wore my good yellow suit," I said to myself, "and I'm glad I got my hair cut last night." Somehow, looking my best while being fired made a difference.

Dreading how the news would affect my husband, Allen, I drove home. I didn't dare to think about how we would tell the kids or our families. Yet in a strange way I was prepared, even relieved. Over lunch Allen and I talked about what we should do—or I should say he talked and I cried. But between sobs I began to determine what I might do. Because no other paper was handy, I grabbed a napkin and a felt-tip pen to list in order of priority the possibilities. Of one thing I was certain: the last item on my list would be another office job. To our surprise, the first thing I wrote down was "teach"; the second was no surprise, "write."

"Hadn't you planned on quitting in a few years so that you could write?" Allen asked.

I nodded.

"Well, it's happened a little earlier than we planned."

Wasn't that a fact—and hardly any comfort.

It was Labor Day weekend, when we had planned to visit the Stratford Shakespeare Festival in Canada. Should we go? Should we stay? We went anyway and had a wonderful time. We walked and talked and weighed the possibilities—yet the list always stayed the same: teach and write. But where could I teach? The *what* I could teach was easy to answer.

When we returned from Canada, I called the chairman of the English department at a local college to ask about the possibilities. He answered as I had expected, "Nothing now, though if I'd known earlier I could have used you to teach freshman writing." He wasn't the only one who wished he had known earlier. "Call me again in October for an interview." So I hung up the phone, resigning myself to home life, at least for a year.

My worry now was to tell my parents. I saw again my sister's troubled face and heard her words. How angry and disappointed everyone would be with me. Week after week I put off writing the letter; I knew I couldn't call. I pretended I needed more time before telling them. Then, a startling thing happened.

As I walked in our door from my final Friday at work—and the most draining two weeks of my life—the phone rang. It was my secretary—former secretary. "The department chairman just phoned and wants you to call him right back," she told me. I hung up, waited for the dial tone, and pushed the buttons. Busy. I tried again, and again. Still busy. Finally, though, I reached him.

"There's a five percent chance I may be able to offer you a course," he said. "I'll know by tomorrow afternoon; registration is heavier than we expected. I don't expect to need you, but if I do are you available to start teaching Monday?" Was I . . .

Forty-eight hours later I was writing my name on a blackboard in front of twenty-two students, doing at last what my mother had wanted me to do all along—and so she said when I finally gave her the bad news, news she thought the best she'd heard in a long time. "I don't know how you stood an office for so long," she said. (My mother and sisters think that working in an office is the worst of all possible fates.) Nor was my father upset: "Probably made some honcho mad. Happens all the time." What happened to "never fail?" They just didn't see this as a failure.

I did—I still do—but I discovered something I would never have known without the extremity of losing a job and being forced into part-time work: I love teaching, I enjoy staying at home, and I appreciate my flexible schedule, particularly with summers off for extended research. I discovered how much I could accomplish writing even two hours a day; during my first year I completed two books that were half-finished and wrote my first two novels. Although the chairman had told me he could only give me one course that year, I taught again the second semester. I also taught an interdisciplinary course during the school's January interim. To my surprise, I was having more fun than I had had since my first year out of college.

And Allen said I was easier to live with. What a blessing.

Giving Up

Not all bad circumstances have happy endings; not all blessings in disguise throw off their wicked-witch costume to reveal a Cinderella. What if I had *not* found part-time work or written anything or salvaged any beauty from an ugly situation? Would I still have found a blessing? Although I can't say how, I know that the answer is yes. I have a friend in Great Britain who went through a similar bitter job loss recently; when I last heard he still had no comparable job but was forced to find work demeaning to his intelligence and experience. Is God blessing him? I have no doubt about the answer, because God is sovereign.

Sometimes there's nothing else to hang on to, nothing else to say, despite how little warmth that gives. Nor may we see what can come of perseverance, which is usually the last thing we want to do when blessings sneak in by the back door. Darren knows what I'm talking about.

I liked Darren from the first day of class and was glad he'd found his way to my section, despite his almost unpronounceable last name. He was not a typical freshman; he wanted to be a chef and eventually own a restaurant. He thought food, dreamed food, and breathed food, which gave us something in common, because I love to cook and find no better reading than a cookbook. I understood what motivated him.

Of all the freshmen I knew, he was having the most difficulty adjusting to what the school called food. The others didn't like it, but he understood its utter depravity. Only a person who knows utterly right food can recognize food gone utterly wrong. Yet the food wasn't Darren's only difficult adjustment. Despite the fact that two of his sisters were on campus, he was lonely; try as he might he couldn't make friends.

"I need to see you," he said as he handed me his second paper. "About *that* . . ." He indicated the paper. "And other things," he added, his voice barely above a whisper. "Will you be in your office at four?" I nodded.

Darren was early, a man after my own heart, and I was ready for him; in fact, I'd already graded his paper. "Well, I see you didn't finish your paper," I said, returning it to him. "Nevertheless, I'd rather have something than nothing—better half-finished than late. At least we have something to work with. You can make it up on the revision due next week."

Although he seemed relieved at this, I could tell that his paper was not the real issue. "I wanted to explain why it isn't finished," he said. "I've been having a hard time." I nodded my head. Although school was only three weeks old, already numerous students had told me the same thing. I'd even had a student on the first day of class tell me he was behind and didn't think he'd be able to catch up or keep up. Even for a freshman that was quite a feat, to be ahead of being behind.

I shook those thoughts from me and concentrated on

Darren. Maybe he really *did* have a problem; many freshmen manufacture them.

". . . talk to me."

"Would you repeat that?" I asked, quite sure I hadn't heard him correctly.

"No one will talk to me, including my roommate. He hasn't said anything all semester, even when I ask him questions. I've tried making friends; I've called people; but no one stops by or returns my calls. I can't think of anything else. So my work is suffering."

This had me stumped. I knew Darren was different—not many guys are interested in cooking—but why would people be so cruel? To buy time, I asked, "Have you talked with anyone about this?"

"My RA spent hours this weekend trying to get my roommate to talk—and I've been to the chaplain. I've even tried to move to a different dorm. I don't know how much more I can take."

And as he fought against tears, I knew he meant it. Well, he'd tried confronting the problem, without success. Maybe he should try ignoring it for a while, which I suggested; I knew he wanted to do well and that grades of C were adding to his anxiety. "Forget about it for now. Concentrate on school work. Think about your research paper; find a topic you'll love." He looked skeptical as he thanked me and left my office.

A few days later Darren was back in my office, apologizing for a missed appointment to discuss his research paper. He'd been involved in another marathon with his RA and roommate and hadn't been able to break away. "I think I'm going to leave school and go home; at least my parents will talk to me."

"Do you really want to do that?" I asked him.

Reluctantly, he admitted that he didn't. "But I'm used to lots of friends—not *this*."

"Maybe part of the problem is that your interests are so unlike anyone else's. Why not stick out this semester and next semester take a cooking course at another school in the area and a lighter load here? Find people who like what you like. But I don't think you ought to quit."

"I'll try—but—what am I going to do my paper on?" It was almost a wail. The area was, broadly, American history; he was Canadian. "How about Fannie Farmer?" I suggested. "You know that she revolutionized cooking." No, he didn't know; in fact, he'd never heard of her or her Boston Cooking School. Nevertheless, he accepted the assignment of finding out and left my office, if not happier, at least once more relieved.

The semester was turning out to be as difficult on me as on my students; never had I heard so many hard-luck stories: mononucleosis, strep throat, car accidents, ruptured ovarian cysts, concussions. Student after student wandered by my office with bad news, all to be confirmed in writing by the dean's office. Although he dutifully attended class, Darren continued to look glum.

When the day arrived for students to hand in sample note cards, I received another desperate visit from Darren, only this time he was not concerned about his personal life, but his intellectual one. "I can't find any sources for Fannie Farmer; I've got to change my topic; I've got no ideas." His throat tightened, and his voice cracked. The first rule of teaching, I decided, was to keep calm.

"Where have you looked?" I asked.

"Everywhere," he replied.

"Could you be a little more specific?" Students have trouble being concrete, I'd found.

"All the indexes and the card catalog under all the subjects."

"What subjects?" I asked. And indeed, when he told me, it seemed that he had tried just about everywhere. Then I gave him the first rule about research. "It's not that the information isn't there, it's that you haven't looked in the right place yet. Try the public library. I'll bring you my Fannie Farmer cookbook; it's got a good introduction on her. Don't give up yet." Once again I could tell he didn't believe me.

The next morning after I made a few phone calls and discovered some information, I called Darren. His attitude had changed. The public library had lots of material; he'd done some more hunting in the school library and found information he'd overlooked earlier; he'd have no problem with his paper. For the first time in nearly two months, Darren sounded enthusiastic.

And slowly his circumstances changed. His Cs became Bs and then A minuses. I saw him around campus with friends. He worked hard on his research paper and it showed. He enthusiastically explained his topic to his classmates, who showed him by their attention what an unusual paper he had written.

Some weeks later he asked to be excused from the next class to help cook for a large conference. It appeared that a fellow-Canadian and classmate had mentioned him to someone who had mentioned him to someone else who . . . "Sure," I told him. Only three classes remained in the semester.

Darren showed up in my office early that day to get the in-class writing assignment to do over the weekend. After I told him what it was, I returned his final paper.

"How was it?" he asked.

"Look for yourself," I said.

"Oh, no, I don't believe it. I'll be higher than the ceiling all day." He stared some more at the bold A minus.

"What are you cooking today?" I asked.

"Oh, it's for a big food conference, so we're doing all sorts of fancy stuff." He glowed.

"Now, aren't you glad you didn't leave in October?" His face answered me before his voice did. "Yep," he said, the quintessential Canadian.

Oh—and by the way—he said I could tell you.

The Hard Way

Kris was near tears; so was I after hours of giving students bad news, from eight A.M. until well after five P.M., for two days.

"I'm sorry, you earned a C minus. I'm sorry, you earned a D plus. I'm sorry, you earned a D. I'm sorry, you earned a D minus." Exhausted, I tried to encourage these disappointed, angry, and frustrated students to do a better job on their revision. I also tried to help them see their problems of structure, focus, and clarity. With some students—the students who don't work and who don't care—I find it easy to give a well-deserved D or F. But those who do work and who do care—and still do poorly—those are the ones I suffer with. Kris was one.

Her high-school grades weren't the tops, but she was a solid B student and an achiever in other areas—student-body president, for example, a leader. Yet her freshman semester in college was proving disastrous, a typical situation. Not accustomed to hard work or study to achieve decent grades, Kris soon realized she had better learn how to concentrate—even how to read, something even the best college freshmen still have to learn.

Kris looked at her paper and her grade, clearly

disappointed. "I worked so hard," she said. "But I can see how you'd say there's no focus. I just didn't know what I wanted to say." Now I was really disturbed, because students who agree so quickly are often those who are the most upset.

Kris concluded, "Like, I had so much to talk about I didn't know where to begin. Know what I mean?"

Yes, I knew what she meant.

Writers have one of two problems—not enough to say or too much to say. She now had experienced both of them, and in one paper. She had so much to say that she didn't know what to include or what to leave out or how to organize it—and the result was confusion, *short* confusion; her paper was nearly four pages shy of the assigned length. I suppose, though, when you don't know what to say, it's better to say as little as possible. Kris had certainly succeeded there.

"What do I do now?" she asked. Her eyes had that defeated, haunted look all students get near the end of the semester, a look mirrored and intensified in the eyes of their professors. She and I were quite a pair that day. I didn't want to say another word, not one more—and she had lost her ears after she heard, "You got a D." Her question was more a reflex; the doctor hit her knee, and so she hit his shin. But she still had ten minutes left of her fifteen-minute appointment, so . . .

So, we talked—or rather I talked—about additional research, restructuring, working from an outline; we restated her thesis, which I told her to keep in mind with every sentence she wrote. We made an appointment to meet again in a week or so, when she had written an outline and spent more time in the library. I didn't have much confidence that I had helped.

My office is a mere cubbyhole, big enough for a desk and some shelves and not much else. With no windows and no ventilation, after even an hour the room is oppressive, and because it is next to a study area in the library I can't leave the door open when I have conferences; talking disturbs students who have come to study—or to sleep. Not only was I tired from talking, I was weary from too little oxygen. When my husband arrived to pick me up, he saw my exhaustion. That night I didn't cook.

A teacher never knows when students will take advice and when they won't, so I was surprised when Kris showed up for her next appointment with a rough outline and a changed attitude. "You were so right about my paper," she told me immediately. "I left it for a few days and then went back to it. I've read it over and over since, and I can't believe you gave me a D; it should've been an F."

Trying not to look surprised, I said, "Let me see your outline." We looked at it and made some modifications, putting similar subjects together to make it more coherent.

Then she said, "I've learned so much. I really know this library—and you wouldn't believe the information I found that I overlooked the first time around. I could kick myself. I mean, it was there all along—the books, the information—and I just couldn't see things. You said it was there, but I guess I didn't believe you. But every time I found a new article or book, I said to myself, 'Why didn't you do this the first time? What were you doing before? Look at all the time you wasted.' Know what I mean? Like, I was really stupid."

Yes, I knew what she meant. When I was young, hadn't my mother read me the story about Blunder, who never could find what he was looking for, even when it was right beneath his nose? The principle held as true for elusive sources for a research paper as it did for missing socks.

"This has been a good experience for me," Kris said. "I never would have learned anything if I hadn't done it all wrong the first time. Now I really know how to do research. Like, the only way I can learn anything is by mistakes. I gotta fail first time or nothin' gets through. That's just the kind of person I am. Know what I mean?"

She had me for the third time. I think that's the kind of person we all are. Without failures, where would we be? Success blinds me, as it would have blinded Kris, to what really needs to be done. Mistakes make me concentrate better, make me determined not to do *that* again. I don't know but what a bad grade—or an adult's equivalent, a failed job or a failed marriage, for example—isn't a benefit in the long run. Kris won't make those same mistakes again.

Although my office was just as stuffy, it bothered me much less then. What a pleasure to hear Kris say what I had hoped she would and to learn what *all* of us need to learn. As she talked and talked about how much she'd discovered and how it had happened, part of me listened and part of me thought of all the boners I'd pulled, all those backdoor blessings I could have done without at the time but that I later learned to say "thank you" for—even for students who don't like the grades they receive but who return to say "thanks."

Know what I mean?

Changing the Mold

I hated red hair of any shade or variety, and I had it. From the time I became conscious of hair, I wanted mine to be black, the kind that has deep blue highlights. I suppose it all started when I was no more than five or six, this wanting black hair. Maybe if I had had regular red hair it wouldn't have been so bad, but I had an unusual auburn—copper-colored, the kind of hair Tintoretto painted. Of course I didn't know about Tintoretto at the time, or about Botticelli, or about all those other painters who loved to paint my hair color. I only knew it was different, and I didn't like it. Nor did it help when my mother told me repeatedly how she and everyone else used to henna their hair to get the color God gave me. It just reinforced my notion of how dumb adults could be.

My hair wasn't the only thing I didn't like. I had freckles too. What redhead doesn't? But if red hair and freckles weren't bad enough, there were other things that made me different from the other kids in my class.

The list was long; at least I thought so. First, because we moved around a lot, I wasn't from anywhere in particular, unlike the other kids who'd always lived in Connecticut. (This is still a problem when people ask where I'm from.) Then, I usually went home for lunch, since we lived close to the school and school lunches cost more than the lunches my mother could fix, though I did occasionally bring my lunch. Also, I hated art class and loved reading. Who wanted to cut out silly things from construction paper when there were books to read? Everyone but me, it seemed. Recess was okay, except when we played games I didn't like or we chose up sides. Because I wasn't good at sports, especially kick ball, which we usually played, I always got chosen last.

The teacher thought I had another big problem: I liked to talk, especially in class, and the notes she sent home to my mother caused me problems, even though mother admitted that *her* mother had seen a note or two with the same basic format. I thought the other kids were too dull to be noisy. Really, the only time I was quiet was while I was reading, which the teacher didn't let me do nearly enough. If she'd bothered to ask, I could have explained the solution. But do teachers ever ask?

I don't know if my sister Stephanie felt as different as I did, but even having a younger sister in school was different, because the siblings of the other kids stayed out of their way. Stephanie, on the other hand, went out of her way to point me out to her friends. "That's my big sister," she'd say, embarrassing me in front of everyone. I constantly complained to mother about it, but she thought it was nice that Stephanie was so proud and fond of me. I knew better; she was just trying to bug me. Finally, I was always late for school, which also made me different, since no one else was late all the time. But mother had a rule: I *had* to wait for Stephanie, and Stephanie was slow. (I still don't like waiting, and I hate to be late.)

I'm not sure I ever told mother that I hated being

different, at least not at that age, though I remember doing so in high school, but if I had it wouldn't have mattered. What can you do with a mother who thinks different means special and was glad of it? Not that she's a nonconformist, just someone who is *herself*, irregardless, as she says.

Irregardless is what got me into trouble that Valentine's Day. Teachers could really bleed that holiday and take a lot of time away from reading. Everyone else loved cutting out valentines, making silly verses, coloring crazy hearts—all-day art class, just what I wanted. Our teacher had made a valentine heart for us to use as a pattern to make our elaborate valentines. One by one, each of us used the form. I recall sitting in class at my wooden desk with the gouged-out, pop-up top and waiting for the form, because I had finished the first part of the task. I also recall what happened when the form finally reached me. It didn't fit. No matter how I shifted the form, my work simply didn't match it. My heart was somewhat smaller than the teacher's.

But it had to fit, because the teacher *said* it had to fit. She wouldn't give us any more materials; she'd said that, too. What could I do? Other kids were waiting, so I had to think fast. The solution, really, was so simple; I merely cut the form to fit my valentine. If I couldn't fit the mold, I'd make the mold fit me. I recall how clearly I thought it all out—and I was equally clear that no one would know the difference.

My plan would have worked well, except that I hadn't counted on being the only one whose valentine varied from the norm. Other kids did notice. It wasn't long before someone raised his hand to ask the teacher why the form wouldn't work. The teacher saw immediately that someone had tampered with it; my skill with scissors was none too neat.

Class stopped as the teacher walked to the front of the room, the offending form held in front of her. I recall the sound of her voice; I recall the look in her eyes. She was angry. "Who did this?" she said. "I want you to raise your hand and confess," she said. The class sat motionless; I sat stiller than still. The teacher stared at us. "I won't punish whoever did this, so long as you confess." Still we sat, but I was thinking so loud that I thought the teacher would hear me.

What if I don't raise my hand? I wondered. No one knew I had done it. *But wouldn't that be telling a lie?* I argued with myself. Refusing to lie was another thing that made me different; mother was big on the truth, no matter what the cost. *No,* I said to myself. *It wouldn't be telling anything.* Yet my second-grade Jesuitical logic couldn't shake my belief that mother—and probably God—would call it lying. As the teacher still stood with the wronged valentine held in front of her, I slowly, hesitantly raised my hand. The other kids stared. I knew I'd fixed myself for good. It was one thing to do something wrong—that was normal—but no one ever admitted it. *Oh, well,* I thought, remembering my mother's words—*in for a penny, in for a pound; might as well be hung for a sheep as a goat.* I felt the horns growing.

The teacher tricked me, though, which just proved again that you couldn't trust adults. Oh, she didn't punish me overtly; she merely cross-questioned me in front of everyone. "How could you do such a thing?" she asked. I didn't think she really wanted an answer, so I kept quiet. "And *why* would you do it?" Well, at least I could answer that one.

"Because mine wouldn't fit it, so I changed it to make it match," I explained. I think the answer surprised her, because she didn't ask me any more questions. I had a feeling, though, that my mother would get another note, and I would get another spanking. By this time, I was thoroughly mortified.

We were a vicious, cruel group of kids who thought nothing of ostracizing an offending classmate. I knew I was in for a long siege of it, because I had broken the code of kids against adults. School was looking pretty bleak— and it would be the one day mother had packed lunch for me, so I couldn't even escape at noon.

The teacher lined us up and marched us into the lunchroom where there was no hiding. When she sat us down at long tables to eat, I knew my neighbors would pretend I wasn't even there. I buried my face in my sandwich to gut out the time. When kids started to clamor for my attention I nearly choked on my tuna sandwich. "How could you do it?" a boy asked. "I mean, raise your hand in front of everyone." "And why?" another asked. "Boy, are you brave," yet another said. "I couldn't have done that, not ever."

I stared at all those brown-haired, brown-eyed kids who were treating me like a hero. It took me a while to realize they were serious. For some reason, my actions made me a good kind of different, not the weird kind of different I had expected. Even the teacher seemed more respectful. I don't remember exactly what I told the kids, but I know I told them something about admitting mistakes or telling the truth, though I hope I did it without sounding smug or pious; I suspect, however, that I was smug and pious. I recall feeling that way, so it must have showed. Maybe I even bragged a little about my virtues, which the kids overlooked in their wonder over my deed. Although I wouldn't be able to get away with it for long, I did for a little while. Never in my young life had a mistake turned into such a boon, as I was all too aware.

I suppose I've been adjusting forms ever since, though I haven't always been brave enough to admit when I've made mistakes, nor have my mistakes been as simple or as rewarding. I shouldn't always expect something good to come through the bad; yet there's still a second-grader inside me that hopes it will be so, because once it was.

And that's the kind of attitude God won't let me live with.

Eighth-Grade Survival

A lot of things happened to me when I was thirteen, most of which I didn't much like. I've always thought how lucky I was to survive that dreadful year: an awkward, snobbish teenager in a new school in a new state. I remember almost everything about it, from the clothes I wore the first day to my miserable relationships with classmates.

But I'm getting ahead of myself. It all started in Connecticut when I was twelve-and-a-half. My mother was about to have a baby, her fourth, and she was none too pleased about it, until it turned into a he—and after three shes. That was March and seventh grade. Then my father retired from the navy, which left him looking for a job, looking everywhere, it seemed, except in Connecticut. For twelve years he had never been around; now he was never *not* around, and the rhythm of our family changed. Although I didn't like it, worse was the fear that he would move us to Texas. I was a quintessential Yankee, a New Englander, a lover of salt sea and air. Forget Texas. Why couldn't he just go to work for Electric Boat like my best friend's father so we could stay put? Not enough money, he said, not enough advancement. Who cared?

"We're moving to Pennsylvania," he announced. Oh. That was all I could say; at least it wasn't Texas. Stephanie wasn't any more articulate. No more fresh lobster off the docks once a year; no more beach all summer; no more fun. How else could we look at it?

My friends at church—the oldest Baptist church in New England—didn't make it any easier. "I hope all the guys are ugly and stupid," they said, the worst thing a teenage girl could wish on another. They almost proved to be right, except that I turned out to be the ugly, stupid one. During that wretched year, I often thought about their words and blamed them for what happened. Nevertheless, those weren't the days when parents held family councils to talk about big decisions, so my parents didn't think to consult me. One day I was reading in my room with the apple-blossom wallpaper and four windows, and the next, or so it seemed, I was in Pennsylvania unpacking boxes in a much smaller room with fewer windows and walls covered with stained wallpaper. Actually, our new house was much bigger and nicer than our old one, except for my room.

All summer I dreaded school, which I could practically spit at and hit from our house. I didn't see many kids my age, though, except for a pretty girl who came to deliver some Fuller Brush stuff my mother had bought from her father. I came to the door, my greasy hair in a messy ponytail, wearing faded black shorts and a tomato-stained pink blouse—pink, and with my hair!—holding my baby brother, who looked like a miniature Red Skelton. I was utterly embarrassed. Much later, when Carolyn became my best friend, I learned that she too was embarrassed at having to deliver Fuller Brush stuff and, because of her own chagrin, never realized what I looked like. Nevertheless, her unfriendly attitude at the time convinced me that I was a pretty repulsive eighth-grader. I was so homesick for salt air that each morning I woke up disoriented by the false smell. Stephanie felt the same, though Johanna, only five, adjusted quickly.

In some ways, I suppose, Stephanie had it worse than I, for when she started school the principal put her in the lowest section, which meant she was doing work she'd done two years earlier in Connecticut. It took several complaints from my mother before he moved her to the next slowest section, then the next, and so on, until after a few months she made it to the top group.

Compared to Clark Lane Junior High, the school seemed so backward. We stayed in one room most of the day, more like grade school than junior high, with only a few teachers, who seemed slow and awkward. The man who taught English told us things that my teachers in Connecticut had said were incorrect; plus it was the year for Pennsylvania Civics. When he announced that there was nothing worth seeing anywhere outside of PA, I was incensed; I think I told him so. Because I was homesick, I couldn't talk about anything but Connecticut, which soon bored the other kids. Before long no one would talk with me, no one but the wrong kids, the kids who drank (already), ran around (already), and read dirty books (when they read anything). I don't know what would have become of me had my parents not been strict. Of all my girlfriends from eighth grade, only one graduated from high school; the rest had to quit because they were pregnant.

Although my so-called friends didn't affect my behavior, they did affect my attitude, which was hostile to begin with and became worse. I couldn't understand how

God had let me down so badly as to land me in a provincial backwater like Boiling Springs with nothing but Pennsylvania Dutch farmers around. I was a city girl, much to my mother's disappointment, because I was developing all the characteristics she, growing up on a dairy farm in Wisconsin, had disliked in city people—not that she liked Pennsylvania any better than I or Stephanie, though she at least tried to make the most of it. I tried, and succeeded, in making the worst of it.

But of all the events that year, one stands out more clearly than the rest. No, not reading *Peyton Place* during science class or refusing to let the teacher borrow my desk for a demonstration or being teased about being big and ugly (all those Germans were *short,* so at 5'6" I was one of the tallest girls in class). No, what stands out is the day I cheated on a math test. Although it only happened once and didn't help my grade all that much, the worst part was my lying about it. Miss Long didn't catch me, though she had her suspicions. The job of confronting me fell to my homeroom teacher who, unfortunately, was the same person who taught incorrect usage and who made that inane comment about PA. He was also a part-time preacher—and I wasn't up to any sermons.

He laid it on thick, really thick. Dragging me into the hall, he told me that the teachers knew I'd cheated, though they had no evidence. He wanted me as a Christian to tell the truth; God knew what I had done, he said. Confess and be forgiven. Well, maybe if my second-grade teacher had said all that stuff I wouldn't have raised my hand. But I knew that this guy wasn't going to preach me into confessing. What business was it of his whether God knew I'd cheated? For that matter, I thought, why should God care? None of this would have happened anyway had God looked sharp about his business and kept me in Connecticut where I belonged. So when my teacher asked, "Did you cheat on your math test?" I said, "No," a flat-footed lie, as my mother would say and I finally understood, because my feet were definitely pressed flat against the floor to give me as much stability as possible.

And that was that. With a sigh, he returned me to class. Maybe because I had lied or because I was so miserable, I became openly derisive of him: sassing, grandma would have said and taken direct means to cure me of it—washing my mouth out with soap. But grandma wasn't in school; neither was mother.

Nothing good came of my cheating, but then, nothing bad came of it either. Although the kids knew something had happened and probably suspected the truth, I wasn't hailed as a hero for standing up to the teacher or jeered as a buffoon or a fool. I continued to behave like a stuck-up snob, only because I was so unhappy, and most of the kids continued to ignore me. Although things improved in the following years, some of those teenagers were still my enemies on the day we graduated from high school.

Would things have been different had the second-grader in me come out? I wonder.

Going Down to Egypt

I knew how Joseph felt. Wasn't he the smartest kid around? Oh, maybe he wasn't the best looking, but who could tell when he certainly had the best clothes? And didn't his father let him know in every way possible that he was superior? A person could hardly blame Joseph if he was growing up a little too big for his britches.

Poor Joseph. I can see how hard it must have been for him to keep quiet about himself. People just naturally love to talk about what they love best, and Joseph certainly loved himself more than anything or anyone else. By extension, because of all the great things his father did for him, he loved his father too. But I can see that he didn't love much of anything that didn't somehow touch on him directly.

Oh yes, I knew how Joseph felt when his brothers kidnapped him and sold him into slavery. Didn't that happen to me too?

Well, the parallels aren't exact, I'll admit, though that's what it felt like the day our '55 black-and-white Plymouth with red interior pulled up to our new house in Pennsylvania. I'd read about Egypt, and this town struck me as looking a whole lot like it, give or take a few pyramids and piles of sand. It certainly was a place of servitude—bedroom furniture downstairs, dining-room furniture upstairs, and boxes everywhere. The furniture people had beat us to the house, dumped the stuff, and disappeared. Because I was the eldest, I had most of the responsibility to help restore order. At least, it wasn't Joseph's father who'd kidnapped him, just his brothers.

I don't think I've ever been quite so miserable. So was Joseph, no doubt, but he was made of finer stuff and soon thrived in Egypt. I deteriorated—rapidly. Somehow I got through eighth grade, as I've described, and started high school with one goal: to survive and get out. I couldn't see the blessings that Pennsylvania would bring; in that, Joseph was a lot brighter than I. Although we're not told that he understood his slavery to be his blessing, I think he knew it. Otherwise, how could this arrogant teenager have withstood his hardships so well? Then, too, we have his words to his brothers: you meant it for evil but God meant it for good. Most of us think he meant becoming second-in-command, and I'm sure that was part of it, though not the greater part. The slavery itself was the good thing, for without it Joseph would not have become the person he did. God knew that in order to reach Joseph his arrogance had to be tempered.

That, I'm sorry to admit, is also an apt word for my behavior—arrogant. I had been a leader, and popular, in Connecticut, well-known, as such things go. (There was a reason why my mother called me Princess Margaret Rose or asked, often, "Does that suit your majesty's fancy?" I was a real pill to raise.) Then Egypt changed it all. No one knew me and no one wanted to, because I had no roots, no family that went back generations; these people suspected newcomers.

It might not have been so bad had my father decided to buy any house but the one he bought. The girl who had lived there was greatly missed because she had been greatly popular. Everybody told me about her; she was my age, and her name was Cheryl too, which clinched it. I, a usurper, a pretender to the throne, could never measure up to the original, not in any way. Although I had her name and her bedroom, I had nothing else. I soon became mighty tired of the comparison.

My wits might have been slower than Joseph's, yet I soon recognized that I had better do something if I wanted to survive. So on a purely pragmatic basis, I changed my behavior. I forced myself to praise PA, to eat buckets of chicken-corn soup, and to cheer madly whether our school won or lost. Slowly, things changed. A few kids became my friends, and over the years we became close.

Essentially, though, my life was a lie. I didn't like Pennsylvania, I didn't like the school, and I didn't much like chicken-corn soup, though I knew I had to become as much like that other Cheryl as possible. Joseph, on the other hand, who had no problems telling the truth, who survived without lying. He could have lied—or behaved in a way that was in effect a lie by sleeping with his master's wife. Instead, he chose the truth and received a prison sentence. If ever a person had reason to doubt God, it was Joseph. First slavery, then prison. Where was the blessing Joseph had been raised to expect? We look at his life, and we don't see it anywhere until he becomes rich and famous. Ah, we say, now he's got the blessing. But did he?

I wish I could say that my adjustment brought me all kinds of good things—or that my lying became in time the truth, that I learned to accept Pennsylvania as my blessing, and that I even learned to like it a little. Certainly Joseph learned to love Egypt. But I never got beyond what I characterized as the provincialism, the stupidity, or the crudeness of the people and their way of life. At the time I never saw what a blessing Pennsylvania was because I couldn't see myself change. By lying I learned to tell the truth; by pretending I learned how false a place it was to live in.

Much later, however, I saw that pretending was bad and that lying, though effective at first, was destructive in the end, destructive to the soul if not to the body. Without going through Egypt, I couldn't have learned this. Did I become homecoming queen or valedictorian—high-school equivalents of my second-grade applause? No, nothing like that happened. The closest I came was to be one of four speakers at my high-school graduation; the other three were straight-A students. That honor came, not because I had good grades—I didn't—or was a class leader—I wasn't—but as the result of a writing contest. My win shocked my teachers who judged the contest as much as it did me.

Maternity Clothes

"How much farther? I'm not sure I can—" With a sharp intake of breath, the woman stopped and doubled over. Her husband reached her side quickly, helping her to sit for a few moments with her head between her knees, which was difficult for her to do. Her damp forehead made her shiver in the chilly air.

"I—I'm all right now. We've got to keep moving. It's so late. Soon. I'll need a bed soon."

Not that she was complaining. She wasn't a whining or a bitter woman, for which her husband was grateful, not like his brother Reuven's wife, always after him for more oil, more straw, more figs. And fat already, after only a few years. The man wiped his wife's face with the corner of his dusty robe, wishing things could have been different for them this first year of their marriage. No one wants to start married life with a pregnancy or such a journey as they had been forced to make. Yet he also was not a complainer, and he knew that for some reason they were worthy of this painful gift of God. Both of them were bearing this burden that lay so close under his wife's heart. Almost, though, Reuven's taunts had jabbed him into cursing the gift. Almost. How often since had he been glad he had held his tongue.

Slowly his wife stood up, put her hand on the side of the donkey, and motioned for her husband to begin again. A few flickering lights in the distance urged them forward. If only they made it in time.

Behind him, he heard his wife's breath come in short gasps. "Let me put you on the donkey," he said. "He won't mind."

"No. Though I long to rest, the pain is lessened by walking."

The man shrugged his shoulders, nodded, and once more picked up the lead reins to concentrate his energy on reaching the village as quickly as possible. They could not risk the village shutting itself off for the night, leaving them outside its protection.

He need not have worried. When they finally reached the village, after only a few more brief rests, the streets were crowded and the villagers not yet ready for sleep, despite the hour. The man struggled his way to the inexpensive inn he remembered, surprised by the crowds and now concerned that no cheap lodging would be found. "Stay here," he said to his wife, when he saw that he would make better progress without her or their donkey. Seating her out of the way, he went to the door of the inn.

It took some minutes before the innkeeper acknowledged the man's knocks. From where the woman sat she could see her husband talking rapidly, his arms waving, his fingers pointing, first at her, then the donkey, then at himself, then up to the heavens. She smiled to herself at her husband's frantic movements. *So hard*, she thought to herself, *this has been so hard on my poor Joseph.* For some reason, her fears and doubts had disappeared on the journey. Now she merely longed for a place to end the job. When a hard kick and a deep cramp brought tears to her eyes, she knew she had little time to wait. With her head bent, she did not see her husband return to her side. His voice told her his anguish.

"He says there's no room. I tried to argue with him, but he refused to listen. 'Throw out another guest?' he shouted at me. 'And what would the villagers say to that, I wonder?' He would not be moved, even though I explained about the baby. Should I look for another accommodation? Or—" He paused. Mary looked up. "Or what?" she asked him.

"Or should we take his stable. He offered us his straw and the warmth of his beasts. I don't know about the dirt, and the stench must be strong."

"The stable is fine, my Joseph. Go tell him. Will this birth be any less messy for some straw and sheep? How glad I am that I brought some clean cloths with us. I hope they'll be sufficient."

"A stable. A stable," she heard him mutter to himself as he returned to the innkeeper, who promptly ordered his stable boy to pitch more straw on the dirt floor. Joseph helped his wife to her feet and led her through the dwindling crowd into the stable yard.

"Thank you," he said to the blushing stable boy, who rushed out as they entered. The place was better than Joseph had feared, though the smell of sheep and dung was strong upon the straw and thick upon the air. Mary sank at the entrance and waited while Joseph bunched hay for a pillow and spread the rest as a pallet. Over that he threw his cloak, though the night had grown bleaker. Mary's maternity clothes, not as warm as they might be, now fitted too tightly at the end of her term. Leading her to the pallet, he looked around for some water to wipe her face and refresh her lips. Only the animals' trough held any water and that was filled with saliva from the cattle. Nevertheless, he dampened a cloth and wiped her face, then squeezed a few drops from the cloth onto her parched lips. Soon she slept.

As Joseph too began to drift off, he felt Mary pull up her legs sharply; cloak and straw absorbed her waters. It was time. Perhaps, Joseph thought, it was as well that they were in the stable and not the inn. He had never realized quite so vividly what a painful blessing birth was, any birth. Yet the Master of the Universe brought Mary through it in only a few hours; Joseph knew that others took much longer.

He cleaned the child, again using the cold trough water, after which he severed the cord as Mary instructed him. She sat up to wrap the baby tightly in the cloths she had carried from Nazareth. Then, exhausted, she slept again.

But Joseph could not. He accepted the truth, and yet still he wondered How? How was this possible? And why in this way? What if the baby died? Lots of babies did. What if Mary died? Hadn't his own mother died giving birth to Reuven? He looked at her anxiously; she seemed all right. "Master of the Universe," he said to himself, "this is a strange way to behave. But I'm only a carpenter, not a priest like cousin Zechariah."

"Someone's coming." Mary's whisper startled him.

"But the law forbids you to see anyone until your purification. I'll turn them away."

"No. It's all right. They're unclean too. Don't worry."

Don't worry, Joseph thought to himself. *How can I not worry? What would Zechariah think of this? What would Reuven or any of his relatives think? Good Jews don't have babies in stables; good Jews don't have anything to do with . . . shepherds?*

Mary was right—unclean just as she was. Joseph sat back and watched shepherd after shepherd enter and bow low, shy yet confident. This absurd scene, which was all so wrong, all so unlike Joseph had wanted it to be, nevertheless seemed absolutely right. *Shepherds,* Joseph thought again to himself. *Master of the Universe, What next?*

What next, indeed.

Losing the Voice

Brenda asked me to attend church with her, and since I hadn't lived in Manhattan long enough to find a church, I agreed. We walked in, sat down, and studied the bulletin. Soon, an usher motioned us to make room for another person. Casually, I glanced at the man and then took another, longer look—Simon Estes, one of the great operatic bass-baritones of this generation.

What a joy to stand next to him as he sang the familiar hymns. What a joy, too, to hear my voice blend with his. After church, he turned and asked, "Have you been to Europe? That's where you need to go to start your singing career." After I thanked him, I told him that I planned a professional operatic career and that I had just returned from Germany—but that I hadn't liked the country. He encouraged me to return: "It's the only place to be." His words brought back the words of an agent in Frankfurt, "Die stimme ist sehr schön, sehr schön"—the voice is very beautiful.

The voice—not my voice—the voice, an entity apart from me and yet, as my aunt warned me years earlier, all of me. "To become a great singer," she had said, "you'll need to serve the voice. It must possess you entirely."

That's what the German agent meant. And to a degree my voice did possess me. The slightest sniffle sent me running to the doctor; the slightest draft made me reach for a scarf.

Yet, though I knew my voice did not belong to me, not in the sense that I owned it, my body, my *self*, was nothing without it. My voice teachers told me to love my voice, and so I did, my singing voice as well as my speaking voice. A trained singer speaks differently from an untrained singer, which also becomes part of the gift God gives some of us. But the beauty of my singing and how I could use it to speak to an audience came first.

Whether I sang an aria, the Verdi *Requiem*, or a lovely, simple Christmas song by Hugo Wolf, the music so moved me from sorrow to delight that I wanted to give others the same gift. But could I? The first time an audience cried as I sang a song of great poignancy I knew the answer. Applause provided a heady sensation, but deeper by far was the other, silent response from the listeners.

Week after week I practiced two hours a day, seven days a week—and worked at a publishing job up to fifty hours a week, as well. All I did was work. And week after week I fought back tears as my voice teacher berated me for not working hard enough. But how could I work any harder? How could I keep my voice the center of my life and yet *not* the center? So during my eighteen months in Manhattan, I came to realize that I could not spend my life trying to keep those two contradictions in balance—for the sake of my soul. I had to quit. No more lessons, no more performances, no more.

Over and over during those last months in Manhattan I repeated those words to myself. I tried to explain it to a friend who could not understand that this gift God had given me had become, because of my love for it, an idolatry; it had to go.

"Come with me to the Janet Baker concert," he asked. Reluctantly, I agreed, but my decision was too fresh, Baker's voice too exquisite; she was doing so exactly what I longed to do, her pianissimos perfect in their poignancy, her fortes compelling. Nevertheless, when I left Manhattan, I left the rigors of singing. Although I performed occasionally for several years after that, and even tried to study again, I no longer desired my voice.

Or so I thought, until the day I sat in the doctor's office as he removed the stitches from the incision on the left side of my neck. "I'd like to look at your cords too while you're here," he said. "Is there something wrong?" I asked. Although I couldn't talk above a whisper, I assumed it was a temporary result of my surgery.

I watched the doctor's face as he moved the light he'd put down my throat. Although I tried to make the sounds he asked me to, I was unsuccessful. Something *was* wrong. "Your left vocal cord isn't working. I don't know why and I don't know if it ever will. Come back in three weeks." Three weeks later, nothing had changed. Three months later, the doctor, elated, said my cord was moving—slightly. I could talk, almost as though nothing had happened, though my voice was undependable, like a teenage boy going through puberty, but at least some of the expressiveness I depended on as a teacher had returned.

"But I can't sing," I told the doctor. "Will I ever?" "I don't know," he said. "Come back in six months."

Night after night I dreamed about singing—or about trying to, for no sound came. "It's a good thing you decided against a singing career, isn't it?" my brother asked me cheerfully. Words kindly meant, words quite true, and no doubt a blessing of God, but words I didn't want to hear, because, even though I no longer performed, I still could not sing with the rest of the worshipers.

Although the doctor said, "Wait," and though a few notes have returned along with my speaking voice, I know I will never again be a singer. God changes the fundamentals, and he doesn't always say why.

Changing Jobs

Riverside Drive at night, for those who love the city, may be one of the most beautiful views in all of Manhattan. The picture window high above the river did it justice. This was the kind of apartment I wished I had found— large, airy, and oddly shaped. In every nook, cranny, and expanse of wall, I saw books and prints and wall hangings, all testimony of the love and professions of these two people, the husband a bookseller, the wife a graphic designer.

Tom loved books—not just religious books, which he sold primarily, but books of all kinds. During that first dinner, the first dinner I'd been invited to after I moved to Manhattan, we talked and talked of the books we'd loved and read. He and I took notes, as we gave each other titles: "You must read this one," or, "You mean you haven't read *that*? Do you have a treat in store!" Kate, a marvelous cook and talented designer, added her favorites. I had found two friends.

That was years ago. Many other dinners followed, both at their apartment and mine, as well as such local Upper West Side restaurants as Shelter, which served the best fettuccine Alfredo we had ever eaten. Eventually Kate and I worked together in a midtown office, and Tom kept my book habit well supplied. Just as they were the first to offer me dinner, they were also the last; we ate at a small restaurant on Broadway near Zabar's, the deli made famous by Woody Allen in *Manhattan*. I wondered what the waiters thought that night, because, true to form, Tom arrived with a stack of children's books—my particular weakness—and I bought them all, a package deal.

Although we kept in touch with too-infrequent cards and letters, and through a mutual friend, we saw little of each other after I left the city; I was surprised, then, to learn that Tom had finally decided to leave Manhattan to enter seminary and the ministry. He'd mentioned the idea casually over the years, but none of us took him seriously, except Kate.

Kate, Tom, and their son moved to Boston when Tom started seminary. They bought a lovely old house; they had their second child, a girl this time; and so their life changed. With each semester, Tom knew that he had made the right decision.

Then Tom finished seminary, the easy part; now to find a church. Although some denominations need ministers, not so the United Presbyterian Church. Wasn't Tom old for a recent seminary graduate? He tried church after church, but whether on its part or his, none of them worked out. He was back selling books part-time, and Kate was also working, more hours than she wanted to. Both of them were certain that this would be short-lived.

A few weeks, however, turned into a few months, which soon became a year. A decision that had seemed so right now seemed so wrong. Had Tom misread God? Because he had no answer, he became despondent and withdrawn; as trip after trip brought just another failure he didn't—or couldn't—deal with, he almost refused to apply for any more openings. Kate uncharacteristically nagged him for his lack of aggressiveness, which only made him more silent. "I don't want to be like this," she said, "for I know it doesn't help. But I've got to break through somehow."

Their strong marriage turned into a difficult one—not troubled, not on the edge of divorce, just uncomfortable, as if their contact was a sore rubbed raw. All marriages have these times, but not, Kate and Tom thought, while a couple is trying to follow God; that should be cause for blessing. It soon became almost too much effort to talk about the source of the irritation. Still no church opened up, and another year had gone by.

Two years is a long time to wait for a job. Two years is also a long time to go without normal communication, so Kate sought the help of a counselor. If Tom wouldn't talk to her about the situation, someone else would. She found a sympathetic counselor—biased, a person might say. Kate quickly realized that the therapist thought that Tom was a harmful influence—harmful to Kate's "personhood." "Give him an ultimatum," she told Kate. "Force the issue. You've got your needs; you can't tie yourself to someone who is draining you of all your emotion. There's nothing left for yourself. It's time you put yourself first. Look out for yourself, not him. If he doesn't do what you want, leave him. You've got no other choice. Let him know that." Week after week this continued. A marriage traveling through a bad patch threatened to become a dying one—and at the advice of a marriage counselor. Appalled by this advice, Kate kept Tom and dumped the therapist.

Later she told me, "I went to her for help in dealing

with the situation, not advice on how to get out of it. But,"
she added, "that's what everybody thinks today. If
something's bad, walk. Don't stick it out. Yet I promised
to do that when I got married. What difference does it
make that I didn't expect Tom to go into the ministry or be
out of work this long? It seems to me I made my choice a
long time ago." Isn't that true for most of the choices we
make? I thought to myself. We can't foresee what will
come and yet must decide despite the uncertainties.
Fortunately, Tom and Kate understood this, or their hard
time might have ended differently.

I saw them again near the end of this struggle; they
were planning to move to the Midwest, not their first
choice, being Easterners. Although it had been years, Tom
and I got out some paper and began taking notes on books
we recommended to the other. Kate baked a delicious
batch of whole-grain bran muffins, which we ate as we
drank tea and talked. They spoke of their move with some
hesitation and yet with relief, Tom excited that he had
found a congregation who shared the notion that worship
is central to the Christian life, Kate wondering whether
she would find work. The tension in their voices had
disappeared, because they had come through the hard
years with their commitment intact.

Yet they weren't the same. It wasn't just their
commitment to each other that had been threatened; it
was also their commitment to God, who doesn't always
answer "why" except with the words "stick it out."

Custody

This is no way to start a marriage, I thought to myself as I sat down in the brown-paneled courtroom. I'd thought it to myself so many times that I'd finally lost count, and yet here we were, in the first year of our marriage, with depositions, lawyer's bills, and court dates crowding out everything else.

For months I hadn't been able to sleep through the night; neither had Allen. Over and over we asked the same questions. Why? Why did all this have to happen? What's wrong with joint custody? What's wrong with the system when a father has no rights, a father who loves his children? What is so terrible about wanting to see your children regularly? Why is there so much hatred? Why?

We talked of nothing else. Although all parents worry about their children or talk about their future, it seemed that we couldn't talk about our future because of our fear for theirs. Nor could we talk about something as ordinary as whose turn it was to do the dishes or whether the Redskins would win the Super Bowl without losing a game—as they did the year we went to court. Even now it's hard to think of football without recalling that courtroom. I had never known that life or people could be so ugly.

Nor had I believed that I could feel such intense anger, bordering on hatred, and it never left me. I was angry at everything—my marriage, my circumstances, my nonexistent legal status as a stepmother, my stepchildren who changed with the time of day—a result, no doubt, of their anger. Convinced that if Allen hadn't remarried none of this trouble would have come to him, I was, most of all, angry at myself.

Would I have married had I known what I faced? I asked myself, but I couldn't answer the question. Over and over I said to him, "You're going to hate me, you're going to hate me." No reassurances could assuage my fears. Since then, I've learned that my reactions were no different from most new stepmothers, but at the time I only knew about my own circumstances. What could I do?

None of the pious answers or the platitudes helped. "Just don't think about it," I said to myself, and so did others, my husband included. It was like telling someone whose hair is on fire to comb it as if nothing were wrong.

"Pray about it; leave it with God"—another pious response. I'd grown up on those words and believed them, so pray I did. Oh yes. I prayed to win. Wasn't that the best for everyone, especially the children? Boys needed their father, all the psychologists said. Some states even determine custody by sex—boys with fathers, girls with mothers. Although that sounded right to me, I wondered whether I would think so if my stepchildren were girls. Nevertheless, I pushed the thought away every time it threatened. I told God repeatedly that if he knew what was right, which I assured him I knew he did, he would see to it that those children lived with us and that he'd change some hearts to make it happen.

"Claim the promise of God that he who seeks finds,

he who knocks will have the door opened." Right—another easy Bible verse to quote but a difficult one to understand. "Okay, God," I said. "I'm seeking and I expect you to open the door; this is your cue. You and I both know what's best here; you and I both know what I'm seeking." Such arrogant prayers. I wanted a blessing, a blessing I saw in only one way—a win.

As he always does, God saw things differently. He looked beneath my bravado, my fear, and my anger to what I really wanted—peace, resolution, an absence of hatred: freedom, for me, for Allen. But most of all I wanted his relationship with his children—and now my children too—to flourish.

I was the child who begs his father to beat up his enemies, only to return later and thank him for knowing which requests to fulfill and which to ignore. God ignored my pleas to beat up my enemies, as he undoubtedly ignored those same pleas from David that we read in the Psalms, which, because I understood them so well, comforted me so much. At the same time, though, I recognized their immorality, and that provided the greatest comfort; if God allowed David to write psalms like those, then maybe I would not be condemned for echoing his emotions.

God saw, as well, that I meant by my prayer to have hearts changed, though I didn't have my own in mind. Do any of us when we pray such a prayer? But slowly, so slowly the change was at first imperceptible, the direction of my heart shifted away from the problems and by degrees toward God. Winning ceased to be important, which was a blessing, because we didn't win—at least not the way I wanted. We received no miracles, no great change in the circumstances, which still remain difficult.

Our relationship as a family trudges forward, some days well, some days stumbling miserably, rather, I suspect, as most families stumble. There have been—and still are, probably—many days when my heart shifts backward, though never as far back as before.

During one of the darkest days, as we were seated in front of the fire to keep off at least the physical chill of that winter, I asked Allen to predict what would happen. "Will we win?" I asked him, those being the days when I still thought and prayed in such terms. "I don't know," he said. "Does it matter? The blessing is not in winning; the blessing is right now, going through this experience and learning what we can." I nodded my head, at the time not understanding in the slightest what he meant. But it was Joseph enslaved in Egypt all over. It was David hiding from the wrath of Saul. It was Adam and Eve thrust from the garden. It was that wonderful provision of God— grace—his blessing in disguise.

Displaced

Looking back over the last few years, Marge saw scene after unpleasant scene. She recalled each difficult circumstance, each argument, each fear. How many times had she heard the phone slam in her ear? How many times had her hopes and those of her husband been destroyed by that disembodied voice? With a sigh, she turned over in bed, thinking again that the situation would never be all she wanted. Despite herself, she replayed the first time it happened.

She and Don hadn't seen John in several months. The first time he had been sick, or so they were told. After some rearranging, they rescheduled his birthday visit for a month later, but what else could they do? A court might say "once a month," but there were many inventive ways of avoiding the order. When the day arrived, Marge thought things would go well this time. Wasn't John's party planned, the crepe paper and happy-birthday signs hung? So what if it was Halloween already. Marge was finishing the frosting for the chocolate birthday cake when the phone rang, and Don answered it.

"You're kidding," he said in disbelief. Then he sighed. "All right, I'll see what I can do."

Marge turned to him, chocolate-covered wooden ladle in her sticky hand. "Now what?" she demanded.

"They missed the plane—got lost on the way to the airport."

"Got *lost?* How can a person get lost going somewhere she's been so many times? I don't believe it." Marge started to shout—actually to scream—and for the first time in her life she burned the frosting. She dumped the mess into the garbage before she called the airline to find out whether she could reschedule John's trip for the next morning and, if so, how much it would cost. As she put down the receiver, she said to Don, "Yes, he'll be here by eleven, so maybe we can still have the party—but it'll cost an extra $40. We're lucky it won't cost more."

"I'll call and let him know," Don said, while Marge returned to the stove to make another batch of frosting, muttering as she worked: "I think it was deliberate. Lost. Nobody can get lost going to a familiar airport." For her, the weekend was ruined, probably for Don and John, as well. Later, they learned accidentally from John's brother Billy that it was a case of too late and no parking, not getting lost. Another lie. Well, thought Marge, what's one more?

As the trips continued, so did the irritations: the wrong or no clothes packed, more missed flights, bickering about schedules, lies, and money wasted because of last-minute rearrangements. And in the middle—always in the middle—stood John and Billy. Not that they were the only ones to feel the strain; Don and Marge suffered too. With every upcoming trip, Marge slept fitfully, suffered from nightmares, and picked at Don for imaginary problems, all because of the uncertainties. Would the kids show up? Would they get another last-minute call?

The children, too, showed the strain. When they did arrive as planned, they were withdrawn, rigid, or openly hostile. Marge and Don clung to the knowledge that after a few days, sometimes only after a few hours, John and Billy would return to normal. Yet how hard it was to deal with the situation, to behave in a positive and nonhostile manner, so that the children could respond in the same way.

Turning over in bed again, Marge had to admit to herself that she, at least, hadn't always succeeded. Don, on the other hand, had saved the situation numerous times; patient, long-suffering Don, who of anyone she knew managed to accomplish the command of Jesus to love our enemies and to do good to those who curse us. How does he do it? she wondered. He seemed to grow stronger despite—or was it because of?—their circumstances. Would she? Would John and Billy?

Marge tried to remember that the children loved them, despite the difficult circumstances. She also tried to remember their goal: to behave as godly parents and establish normal family patterns, normal for them, at any rate. "Lots of families have their difficult times," Don said. They knew that theirs was no longer an unusual situation even for Christian families.

So despite their longing to give up they continued to work to be a family. Over the years as the children grew the canceled flights and last-minute phone calls became more and more infrequent. John and Billy changed and matured, as did Marge and Don. It was almost as if the four of them were growing up together.

Because the circumstances had improved so much, Marge and Don received a double kick that Easter, when after their traditional Saturday breakfast of pancakes, maple syrup, and sausages, Billy suddenly exploded. "I can't take it any more. I just can't take it. I hate being here, and I hate being there. I don't have any place that's mine. I don't belong anywhere." He could barely get the words out, his teeth clenched, his throat constricted, the tears falling despite his efforts not to cry.

Marge and Don had sensed that both John and Billy were unusually withdrawn the day they had arrived, but they had not expected such an outburst. John echoed his brother's emotions, at least about this Easter, this trip.

Marge remembered how calmly Don treated the situation. She clenched her fists under the covers as she recalled that four-hour outburst of Billy's. He had held in his anger too long. "I just want to run away—and I've thought about it lots. Lots," he said, as he glared at his father with defiant, bitter eyes. "I'm going to choose where I want to be. My therapist says I can. It's time for me to choose."

Therapist? Choose? Marge and Don had looked stunned. A therapist telling a fifteen-year-old he can make such a choice?

After Billy and John had exhausted their emotions, things settled into an uneasy normality. Don believed it was the best thing to have happened in five years—a blessing, a true turning point. Marge had to admit to herself as she tried to settle back to sleep that Don might have been right.

Shortly after his explosion, Billy began to change, as though a boil had finally burst and could now heal. He no longer seemed or acted as displaced as before. Slowly he began to accept his circumstances as normal for him.

Of course, nothing so complex is that simply resolved, as Marge and Don learned. That wasn't Billy's last outburst; his problems with belonging didn't simply disappear. Then John took over where his brother left off. As Marge shifted again, she wondered where it would end or whether any decision could be called right.

"Awake?" Don asked Marge sleepily.

"Mmm," she answered.

"Thinking?"

"Yes." She sighed.

Don turned over, slightly more awake. "Sounds serious."

"Yes and no. I was wondering what kind of blessing is waiting for us."

"Blessing? Marge, do you know it's almost four?"

"Oh, all right. I don't suppose it's all that important now if you're not up to a theological discussion. But remind me to tell you about it at breakfast."

"Sure. Now can I go back to sleep?"

Sibling Rivalry

The Bible contains a lot of rivalry—between kings and kingdoms, between kings and prophets, between kings and priests, between husbands and wives, between parents and children, and of course, between people and God. When we look at it this way, it's hard to find a passage in Scripture where we don't read about rivalry. Even those contented, placid, worshipful psalms seem few when they're crushed between psalms of despair, imprecation, or anger.

Of sibling rivalry we find some outstanding examples. People knew how to do it long before Freud. They lied to or about, cheated, stole from, kidnapped, or murdered each other with great invention. Although the New Testament isn't quite so graphic as the Old Testament, even there we have the maddening story of Mary and Martha, a story so unfair that I've always wondered why we need it. But maybe I think so only because I often find myself a Martha in family situations, my sister a Mary.

It should be of some comfort that God's people aren't much different from the rest of us, and it is, though only some. I'd like it to be more, especially when hip-deep in the mire of intense sibling rivalry.

Stephanie and I are two-and-a-half years apart, not close compared to some sisters or brothers, but closer than anyone else in our family. We have another sister some years younger and a brother even younger still. So we were together all the time. Johanna, our younger sister, referred to us as "the girls"—as in "the girls won't let me play with them" or "the girls are being mean to me" or "the girls are teasing me." And so the girls were.

Everybody saw us as a unit, not just Johanna. We were *the girls*. When we were small, still toddlers really, mother dressed us alike and combed our hair alike. Where one of us went, the other went. What one had, the other had. No set of twins could have been so identically treated. Because we looked enough alike, and our clothes and hair reinforced the resemblance, people thought we were twins, a common mistake. As the elder, though, I didn't enjoy people thinking Stephanie my equal. Nevertheless, we were inseparable—best friends, best enemies. (When I was in college Stephanie acknowledged the relationship by giving me a book for my birthday entitled *My Enemy Grows Older*.)

How was it possible to be friend and enemy to each other? We had a seesaw relationship—the same interests and activities, but approached from opposite sides. We both loved books but often different books or the same books for different reasons. We played the piano and sang, even duets in church, not easy for two altos, though she enjoyed one kind of singing, I another. Both of us loved school. What a competitor she was: straight A's or nothing. I didn't care about grades. Even our IQs, so the school told my mother, were only three points apart. Naturally mother wondered why Stephanie made great grades while I settled modestly for mediocre or bad ones.

Nevertheless, if Stephanie went skating or sledding, then I did. If I made snow angels or determined to make the biggest snowball in the neighborhood and roll it down the hill, so did she. We did it, once, a cooperative effort. Our snow boulder was so huge that we needed all our friends to help us roll it down the hill.

But we fought better than we made snow boulders. No one could beat us at it, and no one could keep us from each other's throat. We weren't satisfied with screaming or calling each other names, though we did plenty of that. No, taking the Bible as our example, we lied to each other, stole from each other, cheated each other, and, so it seemed to mother, nearly murdered each other. (Somehow we never found anyone to sell each other to, slave caravans being uncommon in Connecticut.) I recall Stephanie chasing me with a hammer; I reached my room, slammed the door, and leaned against it while she pounded and I screamed for parental reinforcements, though I must confess that when I remind mother of this incident she says, "You're making that up; I don't remember it at all." So much for the memory of parents.

I also recall one of the best fights we ever had—best in terms of ferocity—though I cannot recall its point. I can still see myself standing at the kitchen sink, washing the dishes. In those days it seemed as if I was always doing that (some things never change). I think, like Martha, that I was trying to convince Stephanie to help me or to do some other chore while mother was shopping; Stephanie, like Mary, refused. She intended to go play. Up to my elbows in soap suds, I couldn't shake my fist or hit her; I could only scream—and cry, which I did, because I was so angry. She, as angry as I, left the house, slamming the dining room storm door so hard the glass shattered. How sweet the sound, because then I knew she would *get it*. Nothing was better. I shrieked, "Now you're going to get it! Wait till mother comes home," all that in the midst of crying and laughing at her plight. (I wish I remembered whether she did indeed get it.) What splendid enemies we were.

And what splendid friends. We defended each other to outsiders as fiercely as we fought each other inside. No one could say a critical word of the other without that same warlike animosity immediately being thrust at the enemy, no matter who the enemy was, child or adult. In high school I once berated a teacher for giving Stephanie a D on her first essay in his class. I knew that her only misfortune was in being my younger sister. "*No* one gives my sister a D; she's a straight-A student. Check the records. You'd better not do it again just because she's my sister," I told him. I don't know how I got away with such insubordinate behavior, but he proved me right, because he never gave her anything under an A the rest of the year.

So we seesawed through the years, one or both of us at times screaming "I'm never going to speak to you again," only to resume talking a little while later. If one of us was in trouble or had a problem, we knew we could count on the other one, regardless. I've often asked myself, though, whether we *liked* each other, though we definitely loved—and hated—one another. *Like* may not be the right verb for our rivalry, our competition, our animosity, our intensity. *Like* is milquetoast, and we had a Szechuan relationship.

Our fighting did not end with childhood, and though I remember the early scenes with humor, our grown-up fights have been ugly, vicious, filled with gangrenous, soul-destroying animosity, and I don't know why. Maybe our similarities get in our way. When adults fight as we have fought, relationships can be destroyed, as we have nearly done to ours on more than one occasion. I remember one fight in particular that affected our families and not just each other. Although I recall what happened, the reason now seems so petty. Did I really need to provoke her? Did she really need to pack up and leave before supper? That fight was a long time in healing. Without the habit of exchanging Christmas gifts, it might not have been healed, and yet what I would have lost if we hadn't picked up the pieces. The discipline of habit has saved me more than once.

All of us, I suspect, have at least one difficult relationship in our lives, where we seem to compete not only for achievements but for space to live, space to breathe. With a sibling, the situation is difficult, but rivalry between spouses can destroy the relationship.

It's been hard to see the earth-scraping side of my seesaw relationship with my sister as anything praise-worthy or strengthening. On the skyward side, however, I find a catalog of virtues and blessings. Can I stretch things to say that I've learned how to fight by fighting with her? Psychologists say that's a good thing to learn. No, I can't say so, though I've learned how *not* to fight, and maybe that's blessing enough.

Sisters

"*I just* received word, sister. Guess who's coming to dinner?"

Mary glanced at her sister, a vague dreamy look in her eyes. "Jesus?" she asked.

"Yes. How did you know?"

"Someone told me yesterday he was in the village, though I haven't seen him yet. Have you?"

"No, but we will soon. He's on his way here. Peter told me just now when I went to fetch water. Come on, we've got to get busy. There's a lot to do. Here, you sweep this room, while I begin to prepare the meal. Let's see—cool the wine jug, slice the vegetables, set out the fruit—I wish we had some cheese. Well, we don't. But I can make some fresh bread if I hurry—Mary, what are you waiting for. Get started."

But Mary ignored her sister. Instead she went to the door, opened it, and said, "You are welcome in our house, Master. Please sit here. I'll get you some water and oil to wash."

As she went off to do so, Martha, wiping her hands on her sides, came to greet Jesus. "Master," she said, and bowed low to him. "You do our home honor. I was about to prepare a simple meal, which you will stay for, won't you? You and your disciples."

Jesus nodded his acceptance. Martha, who could hardly believe their good fortune, wanted to please the Master with her home. The villagers called Martha skilled in ordering her household, which she determined to show Jesus that day—he would be willing to wait for the hot bread and cooling fruits and vegetables. Maybe she could send Mary for some cheese.

Lost in thoughts of her preparation, she didn't notice Mary return and begin to wash the Master's feet or see her hand him a bowl of water for his hands. But something caught Martha's eye—the cruet of oil—which Mary poured over the Master's feet. *Oh no,* Martha thought. *That's all the oil I have in the house. Will she leave me enough for my bread?*

Martha hated to interrupt such an important welcome, and correct, Martha admitted, proud that Mary had taken the responsibility but still irritated and worried about her oil. Martha leaned over Mary and put her hand on the cruet. "You have honored our Master, sister. Let me replace this for you," and she took the cruet from her sister's hand.

"Thank you, Martha," she said, unaware for the moment of her sister's displeasure, aware only of the Master, the one she had longed to meet, the one she longed to hear tell one or two of his marvelous stories. No one could tell such wise and witty tales, no one in all Judea, or so the people said. She looked up at him, grateful for his presence and yet at the same time wondering what there was about him that made people want to listen to him. He looked so ordinary—just another Rebbe. Maybe it was his voice.

"Thank you Mary," he said. *No,* she thought, *it wasn't his voice, not with that rough Galilean accent.*

"And thank you, Martha, for your hospitality. We will be pleased to stay. Peter, the others are all right? They have places to eat?"

"Yes, Master."

"Good." And he began to talk to Peter and to Mary—telling them stories, asking them questions. At first, this shocked Mary, though she was grateful he included her. But teaching a woman? No Rebbe ever did that. Wasn't it forbidden? It had to be, since women lurked behind the screen during synagogue. But here was the Master, talking to her, teaching her, so she asked the questions of her heart.

"The kingdom of God, Master—tell me about it. Tell me how to find it."

His words, flowing around and through her, puzzled her at times, because he compared the kingdom to so many strange things, like a widow who wouldn't give up until the judge gave her what she wanted or a man finding buried treasure in a field belonging to someone else and sneaking to buy the land without telling anyone why he wanted it. Wasn't his behavior wicked? How could that be like the kingdom of God? The notions were so common and yet so shocking when the Master spoke them. Mary looked at Peter, wondering if he had heard these ideas before, wondering if he were puzzled too. Sometimes Peter nodded his head, then he shook it, looking as bewildered as Mary felt, which made her glad. Well, glad wasn't exactly the right way to describe it, she thought, but relieved anyway that Jesus didn't confuse her just because she was a lowly woman and couldn't understand his difficult ideas. Mary thought hard, realizing that that wasn't quite right either. When Jesus spoke, his stories seemed so clear and easy, almost transparent; yet later when she retold the story to herself she became confused.

Because she was thinking about his stories, Mary hadn't realized that Jesus had stopped talking; maybe he was thirsty. "Master," she said, "would you like some drink? Please forgive me for being so thoughtless and forgetful." Just as she said the words, Martha brought Jesus and Peter some refreshment. Mary looked at her sister, guilty that she had not been helping Martha prepare the meal for their guests. Suddenly conscious of herself as a woman and not a disciple with privileges to sit at the Master's feet, she began to rise, but Martha had already moved away and Jesus with a motion told her to stay as she was. Mary, though, had seen the look of slight irritation on her sister's face, as well as the clenched jaw, even if Jesus had not. She hated fighting with her sister, which no doubt would happen once their guests left— that is, not a fight exactly, more like a lecture from Martha about Mary's place and responsibilities. And no doubt, too, Martha was right this time.

Again the Master spoke; Peter asked him to explain a story, the one about the shrewd steward whose master had fired him. Mary had heard this one argued about, so she was glad Peter had mentioned it. After Jesus retold the story, he explained it, but with another story that didn't help Mary at all, nor did it seem to help Peter much.

Just then Martha returned with food, which looked good and smelled succulent. Again, Martha's look shamed Mary. Martha worked so hard, and so well, as she'd say once Jesus and Peter left. Then, as Martha began to serve them, she said, "Master, why didn't you tell Mary to leave your feet and help me? You see all that is required to fulfill our responsibility to you and your disciple, and you know what Mary's tasks should have been in fulfilling our obligation. Yet you did nothing but encourage her to ask questions. I too would have liked to sit and listen—but then who would have shown you hospitality? Who brought you meat and drink?"

Martha? Criticizing the Master—or any guest? Mary couldn't believe what she was hearing. Surely her sister was angrier than Mary had suspected for her to so breach what was acceptable conduct, conduct much worse than Mary sitting at the Master's feet. Before he could reply, Mary said, "Martha, it was my fault. Truly I'm sorry and beg your forgiveness. But let's not quarrel in front of our guests. Here, you take my seat and let me finish serving. You eat with the Master; I've been wrong to keep him to myself."

"No, Mary, stay where you are," Jesus interrupted. "And you, Martha, join us. You worry too much about others and about your obligations. Don't you see that Mary has chosen the better part?"

Mary shook her head at his words, for now her sister would be even angrier—criticism from the Master about something that Martha held dear. There would be no benediction for them this night, nothing but acrimony and bitterness and accusations. Yet Mary could not openly contradict the Master; she *couldn't*. Would Martha? She watched her sister, waiting for some response, some outburst.

"But who would serve, Master?" Martha asked calmly. "There must be those who wait and those who work. Haven't you said so yourself?"

Now she was disputing the Master, but with a smile on her face. Amazed, Mary sat and watched her sister calmly eating and talking, all rancor seemingly vanished—not that she was willing to give up her point so easily. What sort of benediction does this Rebbe bring to people, Mary wondered, that her sister, so correct, first criticizes him and then sits at his feet and disputes with him?

Later, after their guests had gone, Mary asked Martha how she dared criticize their guest.

"I was as surprised as you were. But I was so angry, and jealous, I'll admit, that I *had* to speak. You always leave me with the work, always. You're thoughtless of me, not deliberately, I know, but you're so single-minded at times that nothing else can penetrate. Today you were single-minded toward Jesus. I wanted to be too, but—I'll say it again—someone had to think about worldly matters. Did you want our guests to come and go hungry or thirsty?"

"But Martha, it all worked out. You got your turn at the Master's feet, and he didn't mind your sharp tongue or quarrelsome attitude. You were quarrelsome, you know."

"This time it all worked out, I'll admit. But sitting at the Master's feet wasn't the great part of this day."

"Martha, how can you say that?"

"Let me finish, because I'm certain the Rebbe would agree with me. Mary, you and I are different, which has often made me quarrelsome, as you put it. But as I worked and watched you with the Master I began to resent you in a deeper way than I ever had before. I'm sure the Master knew, because as I worked he glanced at me several times with such a peculiar expression, as if insisting that all my anger boil and churn and break through the surface. You know how I pride myself on my control; yet I knew my control would leave if I allowed my attitude to move from my heart to my mouth." Martha paused to look at her sister. "You don't understand what I mean, do you? Maybe that's because you've never felt this way. Yet everyone has things he doesn't want anyone else to find out, Mary, even you."

"I'm trying to understand Martha, really. But why would the Master want a quarrel? That's not right or proper."

"He didn't want a quarrel; he wanted me to release my anger. It was as if I had a deep, deep fester that needed to be brought to a head so he could lance it. Although I resisted, I'm glad now that it all came out. *That* was his benediction to me, Mary, not our conversation later. It's a strange notion, yet I understand a little better now what people mean when they say he does what we least expect or even want. No wonder the Pharisees hate him. Who would choose to know the truth about himself? Or what's worse, to have others know? Even you, Mary. Would you choose to have your wickedness brought to light?"

Mary flushed, turning away and mumbling that she was tired from their busy day.

Martha sighed. "You're a good person, Mary, you are. I'm not, and I know it. All right, let's go to sleep. So, we have enough water in the jug for tomorrow morning? Fine."

In-Laws Who Hate

Samson's parents had the problem and with good reason. Abraham and Sarah tried to avoid the problem with Isaac, though despite their care Rebecca was not all they might have wished for in a daughter-in-law. If blood family relationships are difficult, relationships between in-laws can even be worse, making marriage a difficult adjustment. What does a person do when faced with in-laws who hate?

Jane had that problem. She had married a man who had been married before to someone psychologists call a "crazy maker." Her husband's parents, knowing some of this, didn't hesitate to tell stories of irrational behavior, fights, screams, deep withdrawal, and the rest. Naturally, her husband preferred not to talk of those days, which was fine with Jane, who settled into her marriage.

Then the problem began—a shock to Jane, a shock to Steve. Several months after the wedding his parents arrived for their first visit. Things went smoothly enough, though Jane began to notice how frequently, and with what tone of voice, they spoke of Andrea. They delighted in telling "do you remember" stories with Steve and mentioned recent conversations with Andy. At the same time they began to criticize Jane—or so she interpreted it. They didn't like her food, they didn't like her schedule, they didn't like her clean house. Jane thought that they didn't like much of anything about her. She worked full-time and therefore tried to organize her work as well as she could so she had time to spend with her guests; yet her in-laws accused her of rigidity on the one hand and of ignoring them on the other. They began questioning Steve, nearly every day, about why she did or did not do certain things. Perhaps Steve should not have reported the questions to his wife, but he did. Her response—"Did they ever do this with Andy?"—brought the answer "No. For some strange reason they liked her. They always treated her like their natural daughter, in fact even more than they treated me like their natural son."

"But what of all those terrible things Andy said to your mother? All those fights?"

"Mother cried but never said a word. They just *like* her, to use the words they just used to me."

Jane knew the rest of the sentence—"and we don't like Jane." If she fixed a cool salad supper, her in-laws complained that people don't eat enough meat and potatoes. If she cooked chicken on the grill, potatoes, corn on the cob, and all the trimmings, her mother-in-law complained that it was too hot to eat so much food. If Jane asked Steve to help her set the table or do the dishes, her father-in-law talked about newfangled feminists who don't know their place. And all the while, behind her back, her in-laws were feeding Steve the supposed virtues of his former wife. Jane saw clearly what they wanted, but did Steve? And what, if anything, would he do about it?

She asked him that question one night after her in-laws had gone to bed. "So what did they say about me—

or about Andy—this time?" Jane began belligerently. After almost three weeks, she had grown weary and impatient with their constant barrage.

"Not much about you, except that my father says he doesn't understand you or feel comfortable around you because he's never known a career woman. He says you're too bossy. You want things done a certain way."

"Hmph. What he means is that he thinks I should fix dinner, put it on the table, and then when he feels like it he should sit down and eat it, while the food gets cold and everyone waits for him. That's his control game. And he doesn't like you doing the dishes—not man's work."

"Oh, I know you're right, but we're hardly going to change him at his age."

"I don't want to change him; I just don't want him around." Jane knew that was the wrong thing to say, but she was angry.

"So you want me to break with my parents? It's you or them, is that it? Well, I won't do it."

"No—not break with them—just tell them that you won't listen to any more complaints about me. Or any more praise for Andy. If you have to, tell them what really happened, because you know what they want, don't you?"

Steve shook his head.

"I can't believe that you don't see it when they've made it about as obvious as they can without coming right out with it. Why do you think they've been comparing us for weeks—me always coming out on the short side and Andy made out to be such a paragon of what a wife ought to be?" Jane glared at her husband, willing him to figure it out.

Slowly, a look of total amazement crossed his face.

"You don't mean," he said, "that—that they think I should leave you and go back to Andy, after all these years?"

Jane nodded her head. "What else?"

"I can't believe it, but I think you're right."

"Steve, they've utterly deluded themselves about that woman, and they can't even see me as I am just because I'm not like her. You've *got* to talk to them straight. If you don't tell them to quit complaining about me, I may have to do what my friend Sue did when her in-laws came to visit. She left the house and stayed at a hotel until they'd gone. I'm just not going to sit and listen to them any more."

"I won't have you driven out of your own house, though I don't want to talk to them, especially my mother. She detests confrontations of any kind."

"No, she'd rather snipe at me in her mournful, quiet way."

"I don't know why they're like this, but I'll talk to them."

"When?" Jane was not about to have Steve put it off and put it off. Her in-laws might decide to leave before he decided the right time had arrived to talk with them.

"Tomorrow. I'll talk to them tomorrow. Now, can we get some sleep?"

As he turned out the light, Jane had a suspicion that there were some unspoken words in her husband's mouth, words such as, "Now are you satisfied?" or "Now will you quit bugging me," but she was too tired to discuss it any longer. She only hoped he didn't choke on those words while he was asleep.

After breakfast the next day Steve surprised Jane when he took his parents for a walk. At least they wouldn't react violently on the road. She was glad she had some ironing to do—a good task for worrying or wondering, provided she didn't worry or wonder so much that she scorched Steve's shirts. It had been known to happen. Jane set up the ironing board by a window where she could watch the road, turned on the iron, and began her wait. Steve hadn't told her what he planned to say, but if she knew her in-laws they would find any negative truth about their former daughter-in-law difficult to accept. Yet without that acceptance, she didn't see how they would bump along.

Jane finished her ironing and was just putting away the clothes when Steve came in alone.

"Well?" she said.

"I told them," he responded.

"Told them what?"

"Everything. The truth. What Andy did, what really happened. Although they found it difficult to believe, my father especially, they were angry for me."

"So now things will be better, right?"

"Jane, I'm not so sure. Something underneath their anger made me uneasy, almost as if they were blaming me or blaming circumstances or blaming any one of a number of things, but they weren't blaming Andy. I took my share of the responsibility, but I refused to take it all. I don't know if it helped. And my parents still don't understand you, or us, or why we're here. I'm hoping that'll come. But they know I belong with you and that I expect them to accept you."

"So nothing is solved." Jane turned away.

"Not everything, no. How could you think it would be? At least they'll come back and give you a chance, which is more than they were willing to do yesterday."

"Isn't that big of them."

"From their perspective it is, even if from ours it isn't. I know this is ugly for you—for us—yet surely something good will come from this. Maybe my parents will accept someone on her own merits. You see, they felt—feel—sorry for Andy, superior in a way, and that's why they like her. But they can't do that with you; they've got to accept you as you and not as an extension of their image of themselves. As they watch us, meet our friends, go to church with us, they'll see who you are and that we belong together. I've got to ask you the same thing I asked them: Give them a chance."

"What if it doesn't get better? Then what good will you find?"

"Well, maybe *good* is the wrong word. Maybe we'll only come to understand each other better or tolerate each other more. Maybe we'll learn some patience, which has been in short supply around here lately."

"So, I'm not very patient." Jane sighed. "All right, I'll settle for learning a little more patience."

Silent Marriage

I knew that I was driving the car. Weren't my hands on the steering wheel, and wasn't my foot on the gas pedal? I saw that I was close to my turn-off, because I noted the exit sign—only three-quarters of a mile more. I knew all that, and yet during the last forty-five minutes I had been in a place without language or sound of any kind—no car engines, no airplanes, no tractors, no voices. Why return? I wondered, as I automatically signaled, slowed the car, and turned onto the street that would lead me home. Wherever I had been was preferable to a noisy car. I began to consider how long I had wanted this escape into silence; my husband wondered why.

Although it was a legitimate question, I had no answer, which made him wonder and worry even more. Words were my bread and wine; he'd never known me silent. In truth, I'd never known myself quite this way. Usually I couldn't get words enough, yet now I didn't want to hear them, read them, or speak them, particularly speak them, because lately my words were those of explanation, and I was tired of explaining. So when Allen asked me, "Why?" I did not answer—I could not, I would not. I just shook my head.

But husbands have a way of persisting, as indeed they should in such circumstances, for silence in marriage can, if it becomes habitual, destroy the relationship. Of all the ways God gave us to communicate, for good or ill words are still the best.

"Let's talk about it. Tell me what's bothering you. Have I done something wrong?" he asked after we'd walked in the door and hung up our coats.

Wandering into the bedroom to put away my purse, I shook my head. That's just it, I thought, I don't *want* to talk. I don't want to form my tongue around any words, simple or difficult, nor make my facial muscles and mouth contribute their part.

"*Say* something," he pleaded, as I flopped onto the bed. I couldn't remember ever feeling quite so exhausted, as if even listening to words was more effort than I had strength for.

"So this is it?" he asked. I was grateful for that question, which I recognized as rhetorical, as one that didn't require words. "Do you want me to leave you alone?"—a question I could answer with a nod. Even had I wanted to talk, I didn't know what to say, perhaps the reason I didn't want to say anything.

Had he done something wrong? No, he hadn't, nor had I, but I wanted isolation. Silence in marriage, I wondered. How long *can* it continue before there is no marriage? Is this normal, this longing for separation, for silence? I didn't know the answers, nor whom to ask.

I had heard many sermons about silence—but usually the silence came from God. People who confessed that they couldn't hear God speak and that their prayers bounced off the ceiling in mockery became silent because God was silent. Why would he? I wondered. Maybe he wearies of explaining things to people who refuse to listen to him—or worse, who say, "I'm listening," but behave as if they weren't. But no, that's ridiculous, I thought to myself. God wouldn't behave as I do. So the sermons I remembered weren't helpful. Nor did I know anyone who had ever mentioned times in marriage when a person can't talk; but did that mean they never happened? Maybe they happened so often and created such conflict that people couldn't talk about the silence.

"Let's talk about it," my husband insisted again.

"All right," I finally replied, "I'll explain. I don't feel like talking. There. Does that help? I can't put it any clearer. I've got nothing to say, so I'm saving my energy for something important—like going to sleep, which I think I'll do now." I didn't mean to be belligerent, nor did I say those words with hostility but with utter weariness. In that state, I feel asleep.

I woke up in the same state. At breakfast, I got more questions. Was I depressed? Was something bothering me? Was I angry?

No to all the above; I simply didn't want to talk. It was winter, literally and figuratively, one of my favorite seasons, and I wanted to be left alone to do what I had always done in winter—hibernate.

Strange how that suddenly came to me. Marriage, I saw, had changed the fundamental rhythm of my life in ways I hadn't recognized. I thought about other winters, winters when I stared at the snow, listened to operas and symphonies, read book after book, sometimes several a weekend. I thought about coming home to an empty house, empty of sound but not empty of meaning and of how soothing I found that. I missed the silence of winter and wondered whether it would return.

What dismayed and depressed some people—this black-and-white season—blessed and refreshed me; it gave me perspective, even though this time, this year, it caused me discomfort as well, because to achieve the silence I needed I had to shut out everything and everyone, which included Allen. He didn't want that, nor did I, though I saw no other way. Although this silence came to a focus in our marriage, it was as true for my other relationships; now was the time for my silence, for my recuperation, just as much as for my trees and bushes.

An uneasy resolution began to emerge, one that we didn't talk about, for I never got beyond, "I just need to be quiet." But that, finally, was enough—and to my surprise a new pattern began to develop, one not so dissimilar to the rhythm I knew before marriage; we entered into silence together—into books or music or merely sitting still. Our anguish to communicate, that late twentieth-century demand of a good marriage, disappeared, and the negatives of "Don't talk to me" became the positives of "Let's be quiet together." Although stillness is not highly valued in our culture, we came to cherish and need it. No longer did it threaten our marriage or indicate failure; rather, it provided a respite from the daily demands of job and family. Yet we would not have worked our way through to the shared silence without the broken silence at the beginning, for this new rhythm didn't happen in a day or two, or even a week or two, but took several painful intermittent silences over many months; during those times we learned the blessing of silence and found our pattern together—the benediction of God.

Carolyn

People from other countries and cultures think Americans fly-by-night friends. Once we move, and we do that frequently, we relinquish former friendships for new ones. Like marriage, friendships take so much work that we only have strength to form new relationships.

I protested this generalization about Americans to the accusing Australian. "But what about Carolyn?" I asked, which made absolutely no sense to him. So I explained.

Carolyn and I were inseparable in high school, only four years, but those years seemed much longer than the calendar indicated. We took the same classes, participated in almost all the same activities, showed the same interests. During the summers we went to the local pool every day; during the school year we worked as nurse's aides. If we weren't together, we spent hours on the phone. Her house was as familiar as mine, though we stayed at my house more than her's, because she preferred my mother to her own—or at least my mother's lasagna and apple pie.

Of course, we both knew the situation would change after high school; she was going to a Brethren college in

Pennsylvania and I was going to a nondenominational school in New England. Our last few months were difficult for our friendship, because she and her parents fought vehemently about her boyfriend—and I sided with them, which she knew. So we fought, as well. If my mother hadn't intervened, Carolyn and I would never have spoken again.

Throughout college, we wrote to each other and visited during vacations, but once my family moved to Maryland we never saw each other, not even when she got married, because my exams took precedence. After that, we lost contact.

Several years later, for reasons I can't recall, I decided to get her phone number from her mother. How Carolyn and I talked, talked as if we had spoken only the day before; our friendship was still intact, and we resumed our letter writing. When I was invited to Messiah College for a week of speaking we decided to meet; the college was only forty-five minutes from her home. That week we spent a lot of time together, confiding in one another as we always had. Her marriage, she admitted, hadn't turned out as she had hoped, but her son kept her from divorce. Nor had she ever worked, having moved almost immediately from dorm life into married life. She was bored, restless, unhappy, and trapped. "All I ever wanted," she told me, "was a husband, a nice house, and two kids. I have the house and the husband but only one child." Those were her goals? Although we had been best friends, I never knew what she wanted in life. I assumed she wanted a career as I did, and she assumed I wanted a husband and two kids.

That was almost fifteen years ago, and though we haven't seen each other since, we still write, not often but enough to keep track of each other. She is still married and still unhappy, as she confessed in her recent Christmas card. I've tried to imagine her existence.

Carolyn and I were so alike and yet so different, best friends and yet so far apart, and never more so than on the most fundamental issue of all—Christianity. That was the real rub between us at the end of high school. I preached at her constantly; how she stood it I cannot conceive. "Christianity is fine for you, but not for me," she told me repeatedly. So eventually I smartened up and stopped preaching, but I kept on praying.

Then, after we had begun writing again, after she had been married for some years, she wrote to tell me that she had become a Christian. I couldn't believe the news nor why she had waited so long to make this decision. "Only unhappy people become Christians," she had once said; "those are the ones who need a crutch." Well, she was miserable, but that wasn't why she became a Christian, though she couldn't explain the reason. Nevertheless, she believed.

As many new Christians do, she immersed herself in church, Bible study, and prayer meetings, which naturally led her to urge her husband to join her, but he refused, giving her much the same line she had once given me: "It's all right for you . . ." She also began to read religious books, asking me for recommendations. Her letters were filled with enthusiasm, hope, struggle, and commitment; then this ceased as suddenly as it had begun.

Although I didn't ask Carolyn, I wondered what had become of her enthusiasm. Was it a phase, or had it been real? I've only known one other person who professed conversion, only to reverse herself a few months later; I hoped this hadn't happened to Carolyn. Eventually, almost abruptly in the middle of an explanation of her unhappy marriage and difficult family life—continuing problems with her parents, the death of a sister from cancer, the pressure of her husband starting his own business—she wrote that she no longer attended church or believed any of that stuff. "Or," she added, "maybe I just don't know. I tried to make Christianity work, and I'm still seeking, but it didn't make anything better."

Why did she expect it to? I wondered. Who had told her it would? Had I, in my early days when I understood little about commitments of any kind, much less the daily struggle of Christian commitment?

Carolyn suffers from a common delusion: that Jesus makes things better, that certain things won't happen to Christians, and that God's blessings come with ribbons and bows. We think, as Peter thought, that there is something in it for us—and there is, surely, but not what we expect. Jesus promised us nothing more than a bed without a pillow, a house without a bed (and somehow, despite all that, peace and abundant life, reinterpreted the heavenly way). Carolyn looked at her life and decided she couldn't sleep in a bed without a pillow or live in a house without a bed. She expected John to become a Christian, her relationship with her mother to improve, and her sister to live. When the opposite happened, she decided that Christianity didn't *work* for her, rather like someone saying he couldn't *get* math or a certain book didn't *do* anything for him.

Then she looked at her other sister, a sister who, from Carolyn's perspective, was born disadvantaged if only because of her muscular distrophy; yet she had a wonderful marriage, a contented life, and a happy outlook on the future. Whether Carolyn understands this consciously, I don't know, though in nearly every letter she mentions this sister—her appearance, her intelligence, her weaknesses, and her apparent satisfaction. Between the lines I read some questions: "Why is she happy when I'm thinner and prettier and smarter than she is? What right does she have to happiness that eludes me?" Most of us voice such questions, or a variation of them, at some point, because the answers seem so unfair and we've been taught that God ought to be fair.

Carolyn is still in that state, wanting some purpose but wanting the purpose to bring her happiness, release, and, I suppose, peace. What kind of blessing, I've asked myself, is she receiving? What is God doing with her? I might tell her to go back to church, but church may be the place she received her faulty notions about God. What if I tell her to pray, but her prayers go nowhere? The traditional answers don't fit, maybe because they're all things that *we* do, not things that God does.

Nor can I tell her, in all honesty, merely to trust God and things will get better, because things may never get better, not in the way most of us mean those words. *Carolyn* may get better; her attitudes and expectations may be healed; but that is not the same as her circumstances improving, or of her receiving the kinds of blessings she thinks she deserves. Is that enough for her, I wonder. Is that enough for me, or for any of us, if we are truthful with ourselves? That question takes a lifetime to answer.

Murder Mystery

It had been a hard night, as the sweat and stench and blood showed when Adam returned to his tent in the light-streaked hours. Shivering, he sat near the small fire and felt the blood cake to his skin. Another lambing was nearly over; only a few more sheep remained to give birth. It seemed to Adam that this was the hardest spring in years; he had lost a few sheep before he had reached the herd, but he had saved some, too, with a few well-timed pulls and the mother's helpful thrusts. *Soon,* he thought to himself, *I will not carry this burden alone. My boys will help and eventually replace me, nearly grown as they are.* He sighed, thinking of the days to come when he would not work so hard, and he sighed too, thinking of those days long ago when he had no word for work. Although the memory of the garden had faded so that he sometimes thought of it only as a dream, a few visions remained.

The smoke-filled tent stung his weakened eyes. He could not see either son, who must already have arisen for the day. Adam knew he would not sleep until evening. As he started to rise, his wife entered the tent, carrying a pitcher of water, which she placed down carefully.

"The well," she began and hesitated, seeing the exhaustion in her husband's eyes.

"Yes, woman, what about the well?"

"We may have to move again soon, for I think it's drying up. I had great difficulty getting even this pitcher of water, barely enough for today. Without the spring mists, I don't know what will happen. They're so late in coming this year—"

"Yes, and the lambs so early," her husband interrupted. "We'll talk later, once the boys have returned. When did they leave?"

"Early, not long after you rose to tend the sheep. You know today is the day of sacrifice."

"I'd forgotten. What's the point anyway? The mists still don't come, the sheep still die—two last night—the food's scarce. Even the pot's nearly empty."

"Adam, don't say such things before the Lord. Let me pour a little water on your hands and give you a little barley paste. You'll feel better then."

"All right, but then I must get back to the field. What crops we do have must be tended, and I have so little skill. Where Cain learned so much about plants I don't understand. Without him we'd be hungrier than we are now."

"But Abel understands the animals, Adam, and we need the milk and the cheese."

"True. I wasn't suggesting that Cain was better than your beloved Abel, only that we need them both, or our life would be harder than ever. I'll take the barley now."

After he had eaten, he asked, "Can you join me in the field?"

"Soon, Adam, soon."

The man left the tent and turned toward the east and the field, bowing low as he did, his early-morning custom since creation. Although he had forgotten the reason, he kept the ritual superstitiously. Then he picked up his hoe, dragging it behind him as he walked wearily toward the sun. Along the way he would pass the stone markers where they poured the blood and made their offerings. How he could have forgotten the day of sacrifice he did not know. Perhaps his sons would still be there, but when he reached the place of stones the only sign of their presence was the fresh-spilt blood and the wilting leaves of the offering. Again, Adam bowed low, this time over the stones, never smelling the musky odor of blood, so similar to his own smell. He looked around for other traces of his sons, but seeing none he continued, after another low bow.

All day he waited for Abel and Cain, pausing frequently in his work to scan the horizon, but they never appeared. Late in the day the sky darkened, and the air stiffened, omens that the spring mists would arrive in time to replenish the well, but he needed to reach the tent before the mists were so thick he would be unable to find his way. He hurried as quickly as his stiff legs would allow; he had twisted his left leg trying to turn the head of a lamb inside its mother's womb. This time he failed to pause at the bloodstones, for he never saw them or thought of them. It only took a little time for the mists to soak his skins, which would chafe and rub his chest raw after they dried.

Shortly after he passed the bloodstones the mists slammed against the earth, leaving no crack or fissure through which to see. Although Adam knew the position of the tent, still he feared losing his way in the swirling, wet air. He slowed his pace, since it no longer was possible for him to reach home before the worst arrived. He wondered if the mists would continue as long as the last time they came; they seemed to him much thicker than usual. All sense of time and space disappeared as he walked, waiting to meet the tent head-on, because he would feel it before he saw it. In the distance, he heard faint bleating, but from which direction or how far away he could not tell. Another sheep in distress, he thought—another sheep that might die without the help he could not give. Better that one more dies than that he lose himself trying to save it, he muttered aloud, just as he touched the tent and felt it shiver in the wind and dampness. A thin ribbon of smoke was his only consolation. As he entered the tent, he looked for his sons.

Eve brought him some dry, heavy skins that served as a wrap against the cold and asked, "Aren't Abel and Cain with you?"

"No," Adam answered. "I haven't seen them all day. I was hoping that they were here or that you had seen them. They've never been gone this long before. Are you certain there's been no sign of them?"

Eve shook her head.

"I saw the offerings at the bloodstones when I went to the field, but the mists are so thick I didn't see whether the offerings had been accepted. Perhaps not, and that's why the mists come so hard and so abruptly. Have we nothing more to put on the fire? It gives but meager light and warmth in such weather."

"I dried as many chips as I could today and brought them inside, but we must conserve them against a long mist. Does that matter, anyway, when our sons are missing?"

"You're right, woman. Just let me sit here and think of where they might have taken refuge, for surely that's what happened. Abel convinced Cain to hunt with him, and when the mists rose up so thick they entered one of the caves on the hillside. That must be it. Yet something within me says it is not so."

"I too hear the same thoughts, Adam. You must return to the bloodstones, and you must do so tonight. Can you find your way?"

"Perhaps the Lord will protect me this one more time. Give me some pottage before I leave—and throw another chip on the fire. We cannot shiver our bones into breaking."

Adam ate quickly, scooping the pottage into his mouth with some flatbread, then left the tent. He no longer felt the pain in his leg for the anxiety about his sons. Without them it would be difficult to care for the sheep and tend the field; the field would have to go. Just as he sensed that he was nearing the altar, he stumbled over something and reached out his hand to break his fall. He did not touch the ground but something else, which at first he could not identify; then he realized it was a body. His eyes focused on the face, the empty stare of his son Abel. Adam had seen death in animals but never in human beings before. How like and yet how unlike his son. The features remained, but the spirit was gone, the body mocking itself. Not until now had Adam realized what he and his wife had done so many years ago, and the memories that only that morning had seemed so distant returned in absolute detail, clear and sharp. As he looked into his son's face and saw there his own death and the death of Eve, he cried, the first true tears he had shed since the day they had left the garden behind.

His hands, as he cried, explored the boy's body for some sign of how he died. An animal, he thought—creation gone mad—driven by fear or anger. Yet he found no claw or teeth marks, only a lump on the back of the boy's head. Had he fallen in a fit and hit his skull on the bloodstones? Did it matter? The boy was gone; solving the mystery would not return him to health.

Staggering with the effort, Adam lifted Abel to his shoulder and carried him to the tent. "Cain, my son," his heart spoke, "are you dead, as well? Are we to be twice cursed this night?"

Reaching the tent, Adam with his free hand shoved the entrance flap aside and placed the body on the skins near the center. He turned to see Eve staring at the dead boy and Cain with his head dropped low.

"Cain," he said, "what happened? Do you know? When did you last see your brother?"

Cain muttered his answer.

"What did you say? Cain, look at me."

The older boy looked at his father, fear and bitterness in his eyes. "I said, 'Why do I have to look after Abel all the time? Why can't he look after himself? I've got my own life to lead.' "

"Your own life? None of us has that. Without all of us together we perish—but you need never look after your brother again, because your brother is dead. But you knew that, didn't you." Looking at his elder son, Adam knew he was right.

As if his father had not spoken, Cain said, "I'm going away; that's what I've come to tell you. I have no choice. I—I've been commanded to leave."

Just as Adam was about to reach his hands around his son's neck to choke the life out of him, Adam heard the words of the Lord, and he stopped. Cain was spared, why Adam did not understand. Why this mercy and not the other, the mercy of sparing Abel's life to begin with?

Yet his ears echoed with the voice of the Lord, so that he could not avenge his son's murder.

"Father, mother, I'm—I'm—forgive me. Good-bye."

As Adam watched his son leave, he knew how far from understanding the ways of the Lord he had fallen that blessings and cursings, mercies and punishments, no longer looked so different.

High-School Torture

I thought I would never forget his name, though I have, at least his last name. His first name was Jim, and I can see him still—tall and muscular, yet with puffy features: small, piglike eyes, narrow mouth, weak chin. I can also see the expression on that puffy face, one of utter belligerence and disdain for anyone he did not like, and there were many, but especially for me, whom he singled out for his worst treatment. Although I don't know why he hated me, he made it his business to make my high-school life a misery. Jim was an achiever.

I don't suppose it took much to be an achiever in my high school, since our graduating class only had 120 students. Being muscular, Jim played on the football team, though he was no Dave Butz or Joe Jaccoby; he also starred on the basketball team because he was tall, though six feet wouldn't qualify him for a starting role on any respectable team of seven footers. That took care of fall and winter. In the spring he threw the shot put. He was all an athlete ought to be—a three-season, three-letter man.

No doubt Jim had presence, which he never let anyone forget. I've always been convinced he chose the shortest cheerleader for his girlfriend so he would stand out. Who could miss a six-foot guy with a four-foot-six girl? And she was older than he was. Any guy who could snag an older girl had to be something, because everyone knows girls don't like younger guys.

Jim was also something else kids valued—a hard drinker, a hard swearer, a hard driver—or what is known today as a party guy. I couldn't understand then, nor do I today, why those attributes should be considered virtues. I had seen too much of what hard drinking brought people to think highly of it (that was quite apart from my religious views); I had known kids die from hard driving. The hard swearing, at least, didn't hurt anyone, offensive though it might be, showing a lack of imagination and vocabulary though it undoubtedly did. Yet the attitudes of many adults also puzzled me; they valued those same traits. Jim's parents didn't care about his drinking and driving; nor did his friends' parents, at least from his reports. Why would a father brag about his teenage son's ability to hold liquor? Those were the rumors. The teachers who should have known better, in particular the coaches, didn't seem to mind any more than the parents.

Jim had another gift that made him the envy of so many of his classmates—the gift of crime. He could steal anything, and he always described his exploits in detail to students who longed for the same success. He once stole twenty dollars from me, my entire savings for Christmas presents, which I stupidly carried to school and left in my purse, untended. Everyone knew he had taken my money—the whispers traveled fast—but the principal couldn't prove it. Yes, Jim had it all.

Or did he? I don't recall that his intellect matched his physical prowess. The school never inducted him into the

National Honor Society, nor did he brag about his grades, which is about the only thing he didn't brag about. An incident in geometry class, however, stands out in my memory. I sat in the second central row from the front in the right-hand seat (students in those days were assigned seats) and Jim sat in the far right first row, far right seat— too close for my comfort in a crowded classroom. The late spring day compelled me to stare out the windows to my left; our classroom faced the front of the school and the village street beyond where the cars drove slowly by. Jim's voice trapped my attention in a way the voice of the geometry teacher never could, as he talked about his SAT scores, which we had just received from the guidance office. Mine weren't bad, the verbal especially, but Jim's were great—a combined score of nearly thirteen hundred. Jim said, loud enough for everyone to hear, "The guidance counselor says I can get in any college I want with those scores, despite my grades. He says it shows I've been learning something and that I'm really very smart." Jim had the final quality—brains. I decided not to hear any more; he had been enemy enough before, though I could always comfort myself that at least I was smarter than he was; now I wasn't so sure.

To an insecure outsider, Jim's presence would have been difficult enough—but to be the object of his hatred was almost more than I could bear. No matter what the class—English, math, chemistry, biology, political science, even typing—he was there, taunting and insulting me, slamming my physical appearance, my intelligence, my girlfriends, my boyfriends. His insults were not only vulgar, they were obscene, unrepeatable, and certainly unprintable. He frequently tried to convince my best friend Carolyn that I was a loser, an unfit companion, a definite drag on her popularity. When I began to date a three-season, three-letter man—football, wrestling, and track—Jim tried to convince him of the same thing.

I wonder how he kept up his hate campaign for four years; yet he never let up, not once. Those who have been the objects of such irrational hatred understand the anguish it causes; those who have been spared the experience should only be grateful and hope they never meet someone who loves to hate. That, finally, is the only way I can describe Jim—a person who loved to hate—and who saw in me someone vulnerable to the attack. Since my high-school years, I have known others who also loved to hate, for whom the act of hating was food and drink, though fortunately they were feeding on someone else. I have even known one or two people in the worst of all possible situations—marriage to a lover of hatred, with the object being the spouse.

Looking back, I see clearly why I disliked high school so much. From first to last Jim hated me, no matter what I did, and I tried lots of responses. I fought back verbally, though I was no match for his obscenity. I ignored him, which so infuriated him that he berated me in front of classmates until I could not ignore him. Sometimes I cried, despite my best intentions not to show him or others the wounds he made. I even tried laughing, at him and at myself, as if I deserved the taunts—but that was the worst response of all. Occasionally, though, grace would break through, and even Jim would go too far, as he did in an English class once when kids who weren't my friends finally rescued me, calling him off and surrounding me with "Just ignore hims" and "Don't pay any attentions" and "Give it up, Jims."

Grace, that gift that comes when we least expect it to

ease our pain and help us bear our burdens, whatever they might be—God's benediction and blessing thrown soft as a doeskin mantle on our troubled lives. It does not remove us from the pain; nor will it separate us from the person who loves to hate; but it helps us regain our self-respect and our sanity and see that even in such circumstances we can find the key to God's backdoor.

Jacob Have I Loved

It's hard to understand a parent who plays favorites. Don't psychologists and therapists warn against it? Treat children as individuals, yes, but don't treat one child better than another. Yet it happens all the time, as if playing favorites is inherent in being a parent. Just as there are lots of examples of sibling rivalry in the Bible, so there are lots of examples of playing favorites. When we look at the stories, we notice how often the rivalry is the result of a parent's behavior—Joseph and his brothers, for example, or Jacob and Esau. The disturbing part of these stories, though, is not so much one or both parents' behavior, but that of God, who also seems to play favorites. Didn't he say, "Jacob have I loved, but Esau have I hated?" Why? What did Esau do that was worthy of God's hatred? Maybe God didn't mean what he said.

It all seems so strange, so backward, so upside down, God flouting all the conventions, conventions taken over by the writers of fairy tales. Nor did it end with the Old Testament, for Jesus talks about this same principle in the Beatitudes, and Paul talks about it in many of his letters.

What principle? Why, choosing the wrong guy.

When we read the Bible, God seems to do this every time (except, of course, with his son). God chooses the least likely, the least talented, the most obscure, the most sinful, or the youngest. The youngest is a particularly important category, because the culture of the day demanded that the eldest inherit. Yet in the case of Joseph, God chose the youngest, and not a particularly likable youngest at that—always bragging, always lording it over everyone, even his father, at times. Maybe, though, his very unlovable characteristics made him, so far as God was concerned, the perfect choice.

Fortunately for all of us, God seems to have a knack for turning losers into winners and sinners into saints by inevitably choosing exactly the person we would forget. We might even go so far as to say God is on the side of the misfit, the poor, the downtrodden, the sinner. What was it Jesus said? He came not to the healthy but the sick, not to the rich but to the poor, not to the righteous but the sinner. And Paul reiterates the principle: God chooses the lowly over the high-flyers.

All of this is true *in spades*, as my mother always said, of Jacob and Esau. How else can we characterize Jacob except as a sneak and a cheat? He makes a great protagonist—but a great patriarch? Any storyteller modeling his main character after Jacob would need to make him—and his equally sneaky mother—a lot more sympathetic. Nevertheless, we have the story, with all Jacob's warts and wrinkles.

It opens with Isaac pacing outside the woman's tent, dreading the cries he hears, yet longing for the outcome— a son. What was it Rebecca had said to him only a few days earlier? Twins? "I feel two stirrings in my womb," she had told him. Well, women knew about these things, so maybe she was right. Two sons—a great blessing. Although Rebecca hadn't always been the quiet wife he had hoped for, Isaac knew that in this duty she would prove worthy of his father's choice. Old Abraham had been wise, despite his partiality.

Isaac's thoughts wandered like camels across the desert, until he heard a cry and then another—not the cry of woman but of infant. Dare he enter the tent? He cautiously lifted the flap, the acrid smell of birth strong in the enclosed space, and saw two infants, one ruddy, one pale, both male, lying across Rebecca's flattened stomach. As he approached her, he noticed how the hand of the pale one clutched the heel of the ruddy one, to whom he was instantly drawn. In all ways, this boy was more impressive than the other—bigger, heavier, hairier. Isaac saw the fine hunter his son would be and recognized him as the elder, the heir, a worthy grandson to the great father Abraham.

"Rebecca. Our heir is handsome, so ruddy and strong."

"Ruddy?" She sounded puzzled. "Oh, but the other. See how his hand grips the heel of his brother. He is the heir, the dominant, despite being the younger."

Isaac inhaled sharply, his nostrils dilating, the words an offense and a breach of order and tradition. "No," he said. "The elder, the hunter who will be. He is the heir."

"Isaac, can't you see the truth of my words? Jacob, for so I have called him in my heart, will raise our race to greatness. Esau, elder though he be by only a breath, is too ruddy, too hairy for such greatness."

"Barely out of your belly and already we argue about these sons. Is this to be our life, one of constant wrangling? I hold the blessing, I, Isaac son of Abraham the mighty, not you, a woman and less than my male goats. Jehovah did not make you male. I will hear no more."

But Isaac, despite his firm tone and brave words, did hear more, for Rebecca did not know her place. How she loved Jacob. She petted him, praised him, and provided him the best meats and savories. She taught him to grow sharp radishes and tangy onions, which she used to prepare her aromatic stews. As he grew, he was always at her side, his soft, white skin glowing with the oil she rubbed into it every day, for she was determined that Jacob would not have the rough skin of his brother Esau, who hunted and stank like one of the animals. At times Esau watched his mother and brother with longing; yet he was the elder, the one with the birthright, as his father never let him forget. What did it matter?

Jacob, though, was well aware of how much it mattered and how much his mother thought he should have both birthright and blessing. But how to get them? A vague notion had teased Jacob for some time, that should he manage to wrest the birthright from his brother then his father would be forced to give Jacob the blessing. He wasn't sure why he thought that, but it was a good place to begin. So he began to watch Esau for an opportunity, knowing that his patience and his wit would eventually bring him the birthright.

Although Esau was all his father had hoped he would be at birth, strong, active, fierce-eyed and keen-handed, he had a weakness: his intellect was not as sharp as his eye. He was slow to reason and quick to act without thinking, the opposite of shrewd-witted Jacob, who did nothing without weighing the advantages. In that, he took after his mother who knew a bargain when she saw one, which was why, after tasting the gold jewelry Abraham's servant offered, she willingly left her family to marry Isaac.

Esau's habit of leaving early to hunt and returning late provided Jacob with the opportunity he sought. Day after day, he waited for hungry, impatient Esau to return—and waited with some of the sauciest stew he could concoct. The aroma of lentils and onions simmering in rich broth tantalized him, but he would not eat, because this was to be Esau's temptation. As the days went by, he saw how his brother sniffed and stared on his way to the tents. Each day Esau slowed a little more as he passed Jacob and his food. Then, on a day Esau returned frustrated and empty-handed, he begged his brother for food from the pot. With his usual impatience, he cried, "Give me food or I'll die."

"Not so fast, older brother," said Jacob. "Food is hard to come by, as you yourself know, and there may only be enough for one." As Esau started to protest, Jacob continued. "However, if you are, as you say, near to perishing, I will sell you my food for your—let me see— why for your *birthright*. Yes, I think that will be an acceptable payment."

What an obvious trap, as any reader knows. Who could fall for such an argument? Esau, that's who. Had he truly been dying, his response would make a modicum of sense. "My birthright?" he asked. "Well, what difference will it make if I'm dead. It's yours—now hand over the pot." And so sneaky Jacob got the birthright from foolish Esau.

The glee with which he told his mother of the episode was short-lived, for she told him that birthrights were all well and good but what mattered was the blessing, which gave the receiver the land, the tents, the wells, the servants, and everything else besides. No, Jacob needed the blessing. His only satisfaction was that if he could fool Esau maybe he could also fool his father; Rebecca knew they could.

It wasn't long before blind Isaac decided to bless Esau and asked his son to make him a savory stew from the wild game he loved; after he ate it, he would bless Esau. Delighted, Esau left, certain that he would soon return with the game. Rebecca had other ideas.

"Son," she whispered to Jacob. "Now's our chance. Kill a kid, which we'll cook with wild herbs, and take it to your father, telling him you are Esau. He'll eat the stew, bless you, and then you'll have it all, just as I always said you would."

"But mother," Jacob protested, "father still can use his hands, and you know what a quick nose he has. Once he touches my face or arms—or takes a whiff of my clothes—he'll know I'm not Esau."

"Jacob, don't argue with me. Just kill the kid, while I take care of the rest."

While he was gone, Rebecca made arm and face coverings from animal skins, then rolled a robe of Jacob's in dung and dirt. When he returned with the meat, she threw it in her already heated pot and said, "Put these on. Isaac will never know you." She put another handful of wild herbs into the pot. "These will somewhat disguise the tameness of the meat. Watch for your brother. He must not return too soon."

It was as much as Jacob could do to put on the filthy clothes and wait until the stew and bread were ready. When the aroma was heady and ripe, his mother thrust a bowl in his hand. "Now. Take this to your father's tent. And do not fail. You will not have another chance."

As calmly as he could, Jacob walked into Isaac's presence. Altering his voice, he said to his father, "I have done as you asked and have returned with your stew. Eat, that I may be blessed."

"So soon? I didn't expect you for some time."

"Jehovah gave me good hunting," Jacob said, shuddering slightly at the blasphemy.

Something in the response, or in Jacob's tone, puzzled Isaac. "Come closer, my son. You sound more like the soft one than my own Esau. Let me touch you."

Timidly, Jacob went toward his father, holding out the bowl. Isaac felt his son's face, the bridge of his nose and eyebrows, his mouth, his skin-covered chin and cheek. As his hands moved to Jacob's arms and hands, a worried look showed on his face. He sniffed deeply. "Put the bowl in my hands. Although you resemble Jacob, the scent and the hair is Esau. You've done well, my son."

"Thank you, father," said Jacob, not daring to release the relief he felt. Yet he wondered: Did Isaac know or suspect and yet choose to ignore the lie? Did he secretly admire the cunning and trickery? Although Jacob longed to ask, he could not. After Isaac finished the stew, he placed his hand under Jacob's thigh and recited the blessing. At long last, Jacob had it all.

Later, when Esau returned with his stew, Isaac knew the certain trickery of his younger son. Esau would not believe both birthright and blessing were gone. "Please, father, bless me as well. Is there nothing left for me? Nothing at all?"

"No" was all Isaac could reply. And yet some words came to him, words that sounded in Esau's ears like so many curses. Yahweh had deserted him; his brother and mother hated and tricked him; and his father would not assure his future. With nothing left, Esau determined to kill Jacob.

But even there he was thwarted, for Jacob escaped to his Uncle Laban's. As the years went by and Jacob failed to return, Esau learned something of blessing and cursing. He accepted that Yahweh had chosen his brother as firstborn and patriarch but understood that such a blessing might be more pain than pleasure. He also learned the peace of knowing the place Yahweh designs for his people, so that he longed for the return of his brother to share with him the wisdom he knew. On the day the messenger arrived, Esau was ready for the reunion.

Your Soldier's Wife

So Jacob didn't behave very well in this story. Wouldn't he have received the blessing without his trickery? Probably, but would he have learned what he needed to learn without meeting someone even sneakier than he? When Jacob met his Uncle Laban, he met his match. Nor would Esau have been as blessed had things gone his way. It seems that wherever we look in the Bible or in life we meet this peculiar paradox.

But Jacob didn't really *sin*, did he? A small lie, perhaps, but nothing as serious as Cain killing Abel or David committing adultery with Bathsheba. No matter how we try, when it comes to those major sins we find it difficult to reconcile them with the notion of blessing, because it seems so utterly contrary to God's holiness that he might use sin. Yet there it is, the king close to God's heart, the giant of the Old Testament, David, behaving as wickedly as anyone before or since. And what does God do? Let's find out.

It's tough to be king; life looses its edge fast when he is the center of the universe. Would he like a fig or a pomegranate? He's only to speak the word. Thirsty? Some honeyed wine would soothe the parched patch in his throat. No, don't stir yourself. One of the servants will bring just the right blend at the correct temperature. That day when he left his father's sheep, little did he imagine such a life or that such a life would come to bore him. Oh, for something new.

David wandered through his courts, so familiar with the turns and balconies that he never noticed where he walked any more. On a particularly sultry evening David, unable to sleep, once again wandered through his domain. Although guards bowed and soldiers saluted, he paid no attention, never pausing in his aimless meanderings, until the oppressive air forced him to rest. He leaned his arms against a railing and looked down, surprised by where he was and what he saw—the woman's bath and someone removing her clothes. Automatically he shrank back so as not to be seen and turned his face, but her form, as she languidly stretched her arms high above her head for the servant to remove her robe, made him look again. Here was something new, something fresh, something untried. He gazed at the unknown woman, determined to find out who she was and to have her, no matter what.

David returned to the throne room and asked a few discreet questions of his servants. The answers troubled him, for he had not thought she would be any more difficult to consume than his favorite fig or drink. Married—and to one of his lieutenants. But was that really so difficult a thing to manage? he thought to himself. Didn't he, as king, have a duty to his people to bring them safety and to use his best soldiers in the people's defense? He himself couldn't always be expected to lead the charge or to put himself in danger, not when the heir was still so immature. There were many casualties in war, particularly those fighting in the front lines, where the officers must lead. David sighed, regretting the necessity of war and the certain deaths, but he had no choice. His scouts told him that the Israelites were being driven back.

"Bring me Uriah," he ordered his servant, "immediately."

Soon the trembling soldier bowed before his king. *What have I done?* Uriah wondered to himself. *What offense have I caused?* Soldiers and palace dignitaries knew how testy David had become, almost as testy as the late Saul had been. "I wouldn't be king for all the gold in the kingdom," more than one soldier had said, shuddering at the change that had come over the once-carefree shepherd boy.

Uriah waited for word to rise, his limbs aching from their awkward pose, his back feeling the strain of muscles stretched to their limit as he kept his forehead against the floor. How glad he was that the guard had insisted he leave his sword at the door; no one entered the king's presence armed. Oh, how like Saul was David becoming.

David stared at the soldier, seeing the man's broad back broken and bloody. Shaking the blood from his eyes, David whispered to himself, "I have no choice; the war demands the sacrifice." The servants heard the words and did not understand. Although Uriah knew the king had spoken, he could not catch the meaning. Was that the signal? he wondered; but, no, the words were too softly spoken. The king talked only to himself.

"Uriah." David walked forward and touched the soldier's shoulder. "Why do you prostrate yourself so? A man of rank and prowess should stand erect. I have need of you—all Israel does." As Uriah rose, David continued speaking. "I have heard the reports of your skill in battle. You know the war falters. I am this day relieving Ephram of command and sending you in his place. He has been cowardly in leading the charge, holding himself back. A commander should take the first line of battle as all Israelite commanders have done—as even the kings have done, as Saul, as I. May Yahweh grant you great victories that you return to be richly rewarded for your service to him and to his people." David turned and walked back to the throne; the guard motioned Uriah to be gone.

"I had no choice," David again whispered aloud, not knowing that he spoke. That evening he sent for Bathsheba.

Day after day, David waited for the reports; night after night, he sent for the woman, who never seemed to satisfy him, no matter what she did. David slept too little, ate too little, drank too much. The day came, however, when the scouts reported a great battle and Uriah dead. "Our troops are near revolt—no leader, no purpose, the number of dead increasing daily," the scouts told the king. "This is my fault," he answered. "I should never have sent such an inexperienced commander to the front. Yes, I can admit my lack of judgment. Uriah was a mistake, but—now he is dead. Tell Ephram he may have back his command, with the king's apologies and gifts for the insult in removing him from the field. Now leave me. I will order the gifts sent immediately."

David, haggard from his ordeal, leaned back against his throne. "A widow," he thought. "Now she is free at last."

"Bring me food for two—no, nothing but water to drink. And send for the wife of the Hittite. As I am responsible for her husband's death, I will tell her myself after we eat." The guard motioned the servant to do as the king wished; he was well-trained to keep his face expressionless, though he could not believe that the king was so besotted as to think that his actions were not understood. Yet who dared confront the king with the truth?

Waiting in the women's quarters, Bathsheba had already heard of her husband's death. Soon, she knew, the king would send for her, so her servants bathed her in rich-scented water, dressed her hair, and laid fresh clothes before her. When the messenger arrived, Bathsheba was prepared and dutifully followed, eyes lowered, face blank, mind full of questions. Would she become his wife? How long would he wait? Although certain of her hold on the king, nevertheless she worried that the stench of his crime would reach even his nostrils, forcing him to forsake her—and then what would become of the beautiful Bathsheba? Yet she counted on the king's refusal to see himself and the fear of his people to help him do so.

As she entered his presence, she bowed low and waited for a signal to rise, much as Uriah had done so many days ago. She did not wait as long as he. As he touched her shoulder, she stood, glancing quickly around to see that they were alone.

"Bathsheba," David began. "Beloved. Your husband has died in the service of Yahweh. Because I am to blame—I who sent him to lead the battle—I give you this sad tale of his bravery and valor."

"My lord," said Bathsheba. "Thank you for these words that honor me and the house of the Hittite." Then she waited.

David led her to a bench near the throne, where they sat. Bathsheba would not look at the king, and he could look at nothing but her. *I must speak,* he thought to himself. *And yet how long must we wait before wedding? Will we cause scandal with our haste, which it must be, for already I see the swell of my son begin to show?* He placed his hand where his eyes lingered, and at his touch Bathsheba stirred.

"Should we not announce our marriage, Bathsheba?"

"I am my lord's servant, to whom you say 'come' and I come or 'go' and I go."

"Then I say that the priest will perform the ritual, as soon as all may be readied. Today I will give the command."

"My lord, I am your servant; yet grant that I may leave your presence to mourn my dead, now and until the time of my mourning shall be ended."

"So be it."

And Bathsheba left her lord's presence, in mourning and in safety, for now she was the king's.

David counted the days and at their end he took Bathsheba as his wife. When their son was born, he loved him deeply. And still no one dared confront the king with his deed. Except for the fear of that one thing, Bathsheba lived contented, nor would she have feared at all, for the will of the king was preeminent, except for a certain prophet, Nathan by name. Of all the king's advisors, he alone, Bathsheba knew, had the courage and the wisdom to make the king hear his guilt. But did Nathan know?

Bathsheba was right to fear the prophet; his loyalty was not to the king but to Yahweh, who commanded Nathan to tell David the truth. Wily and wise was Nathan, knowing that confrontation would fail but subtlety might bring the king to his knees. David loved stories, and

Nathan knew a good one. His request to see the king was granted at once.

"My lord," began Nathan. "Allow me to tell you a tale from a far country." The king nodded his assent.

"Once there were two men in a certain town, one rich, the other poor. The rich man had fields and flocks, ewes and lambs, so many he could not count them all. But the poor man—ah, the poor man—what did he have to compare with such riches? Only a small, insignificant ewe, which he loved as a daughter. He raised it and fed it and cared for it, he and his children. This lamb was all to him and all to his children, who had never owned any beautiful thing. For indeed this ewe had grown into a beauty. The poor man shared his plate and cup, and even his bed, with the glorious sheep, who bleated and mourned when out of the poor man's sight.

"Now a certain traveler came to visit the rich man, which all the village knew, for seldom did the people see a stranger. The villagers waited for the rich man to open his home to the man to celebrate his visit with great hospitality, as was proper. Each one speculated as to what meats and breads and cheeses, what figs and radishes, they would eat. But they had forgotten how mean-spirited the rich man had grown from spending all his days counting his cattle and hoarding his wealth. No longer could he bear to part with even the weakest of his flock.

"And now, my lord, comes the hardest part of the tale to tell. For this man, so rich, sent a servant in the darkest night to steal the poor man's only joy. The sheep was slaughtered and served, even before its owner discovered the crime."

Nathan ceased speaking. "Is that all?" David asked.

"That is all, my lord. What more would you have?"

"Why, justice—retribution. Why tell me such a tale unless you also tell me of the rich man's punishment. Surely he would have paid at least four times over for the poor man's animal. Never have I heard a tale of a man without pity. Indeed, payment would be too insignificant for such a deed. Tell me, instead, of the man's death."

"But I cannot lie, my lord. The man flourishes as ever."

"No, this is impossible. I must hear of his death."

"My lord, I would be telling of your own."

"My own? Mine?"

"Yes, your death. Do you not know yourself? Nevertheless, the Lord does. For your deed with Bathsheba he requires retribution, just as you would the rich man in my story. He gave you the kingdom, but it was not enough, was it, rich man?"

David sat still for a few moments, while Nathan watched his face and waited for the king to speak.

"Say no more," David said. "I have sinned against Yahweh. I have sinned."

Nathan saw the king and knew his repentance was true, just as Yahweh had told him it would be.

"David, although the Lord has removed your sin and you will not die, nevertheless he will have justice. What you have done in secret will be done to you in public. What you have done with the sword against the house of the Hittite will be done to your house. And the child you love shall die. Hear the word of the Lord."

So David bowed his head and wept.

While his child lay dying, the child he loved, he would neither eat nor cease his weeping. Yet the Lord did as he promised.

After the boy's death, what comfort could Bathsheba

have? She and the king had killed their son, a son who should never have been. Yahweh was cruel, she believed, to so punish an innocent child for their misdeeds. David, though, seemed content with the Lord, how she couldn't understand. No sooner had they wrapped a shroud around the boy than he called for food and drink; his mourning had ended. Not so for Bathsheba.

David tried to comfort her, to help her forget the one who lay dead. Not until Bathsheba again felt a stirring in her womb did she cease her weeping. This one, she felt sure, would not die; Yahweh would not be so cruel again.

David received the news joyfully, for he too sensed that the Lord would love this son—Solomon they would name him. David saw far when he saw Solomon, a wise man, a man who would give his seed to the nation, which would blot out the shame of his father's adultery and murder. David did not understand why he and not another of his sons would bring salvation to the world. *A strange wisdom,* David thought, *to bless my adulterous union in such a way. Yahweh enters through the rear of the tent—a hard way, and not one any but he would choose. Praise be to God.*

Closer Than a Brother

Many things keep us from God or from accepting his ways, so that few of us can say with Eli, "He is the Lord; let him do what is good in his eyes." When we recently reread the story of Eli and Samuel, that phrase disturbed me. Because Eli, the nearly blind prophet of the Lord, had failed to restrain the wickedness of his sons, God called him to account: He and his house were doomed. As Samuel told him the word of the Lord, Eli didn't accuse God of injustice, as I would have done; nor did he excuse himself as an old man who should not be held responsible for the behavior of his grown sons. No, he responded as Mary had also done to a shocking word from God, in utter submission: "He is the Lord; let him do what is good in his eyes."

Most of us most of the time say something quite the reverse to God: "You are the Lord; yet do what is right in *our* eyes." Bless us *our* way, we whine. Don't judge us or condemn us. Aren't all opinions equally valid? we argue with God. But he is not a late-twentieth-century American; he is not the president, elected by our pleasure and holding office by our whim; and he is not neutral, not at all. He is the Lord and he does what is good in his eyes, without asking our advice, even if we can't see the act as good. Humanly speaking, surely Eli couldn't think it good that he and his sons die, with none left to carry on their name. And yet—and yet it *was* good to God, so how couldn't it ultimately be good to Eli? Wasn't Eli about to experience the harshest of all backdoor blessings?

Some of us struggle all our lives just to get to the first part of Eli's response, "He is the Lord," without ever reaching the second part, "let him do what is good in his eyes." Although God wants us to be able to say both, perhaps he understands and accepts that for some of us the first part is all we can manage. I have a close friend who struggles deeply to say those words. His is an unusual circumstance, surely, the why of his struggle like nothing most of us will ever experience, but the struggle itself is common to us all, if we're honest.

Jack and Joe, identical twins, inseparable twins, best buddies, closest allies, partners. Where one went the other went. What one did the other did. They fished together, they hunted together, they trapped together. With them, no sibling rivalry existed, because they were more than siblings—they were one half of the other. Then, one day, all that changed; Jack had schizophrenia.

He was a classic case. He talked wildly, fluctuating between obsessions, and as his grip on reality faded he suffered from delusions. Jack was no longer the same person Joe had fished and hunted with. Jack was nobody he knew at all. Because Jack's wife felt the same, she divorced him and took his son. Nor could he work, which meant that Joe and his sisters needed to support him. Doctors and medicine are costly, as is hospital care. And occasionally Jack needed to be hospitalized. It was difficult, too, to ensure that Jack stayed on his medication, which kept away the nightmares and obsessions that twisted his reality. When Joe watched his brother, he knew that half of him had died.

Joe also knew the fears, the why-Jack-and-not-me questions. Reading about the disease, Joe learned that in identical twins there is a fifty-fifty chance the other twin will also become schizophrenic. Although it didn't happen, the fears were there, the statistics were there.

But where was God? To a question like that, in a circumstance like that, the glib answer will not do; perhaps there is no answer, other than the answer Eli gave to Samuel, though it took Eli a lifetime of practice to say it. Did God hate Jack that he allowed such a thing to happen? Did he love Joe more because he only had to watch it happen to his brother? Or did God have no part in this at all, just a circumstance, an unfortunate circumstance, more difficult than some, but not so different than others. I don't have the answers, nor does Joe; he just struggles to believe that somehow in some way God is. That's all. God is. Or in Eli's words, "He is the Lord."

Over the years of this burden the circumstances have improved for Jack, which has made Joe hope that his brother would return to work and some kind of normal life. But something has always brought him up short, always another setback. The hope still remains for Jack himself that he will improve, as he does, through medication. But often a schizophrenic fools himself into thinking he is cured and so no longer needs his prescription. No cure exists, however, only a respite with drugs. Without them, the downward spiral of delusions and obsessions begins again, and so do the doubts, the anguish, the bitterness, the hurt. Perhaps watching a loved one die is easier than seeing him trapped in a living death that neither you, nor he, nor the doctors can cure.

Nothing triumphant, nothing miraculous has come from this circumstance—and probably nothing will. Jack will always be schizophrenic, Joe will always suffer when he sees his brother or talks to him. Nothing can replace that relationship. Not that good can't come—isn't coming—but it isn't the kind of good any of us would choose, for there doesn't seem to be anything in it but suffering. Is Joe learning patience? Or acceptance? Is he learning to treasure his relationships? I don't know, because he never speaks of his brother; yet to me Joe is someone who knows how to bear a burden with quiet strength. Although worship is hard, he tries, thus in his own way forming the words, "He is the Lord." I do not know if he can say "let him do what is good in his eyes"; I cannot always say them in my circumstances, which are far easier than his. Yet I know that in some way, if he or I or any of us truly say "He is the Lord," we are also saying, at least implicitly, "let him do what is good in his eyes."

The End of Hope

I first met Stan at a friend's apartment in Manhattan, and I liked him immediately. He was warm, intelligent, and best of all, bookish. He ran the Logos bookstore in Midtown Manhattan, only a few blocks from my office in the Time-Life Building. But his profession didn't make him bookish; his love of books, all kinds, all varieties, did. That evening is a fond remembrance of laughter, ideas, good food, and good talk.

Although we both lived in Manhattan, we saw little of each other during the eighteen months I lived in the city. After I moved into the world of book publishing, we saw each other more frequently, particularly at conventions, where he bought and I sold. Then I heard some startling news—he had decided to leave retail sales to publish what others would now buy. A large mass-market house in Manhattan wanted to begin a line of religious books; Stan would be the first editor. The bookstore business lost a fine retailer, but the publishing world gained a book lover.

I watched the development of his imprint with interest. The company obviously wanted to make it successful for the advertising budget was large. Stan was buying some interesting and broad-ranging books for mass market, some of which deserved a wider audience than they had yet achieved. I cheered from the sidelines.

Then I heard from several friends, one of whom was in Stan's prayer cell at a Manhattan Episcopal church, that Stan was no longer with the company. This began years of suffering for him that seemed to have no purpose or redemption.

Searching for a job in mid-life is never easy, but for Stan it was particularly painful, because at the same time he learned that he had a brain tumor. The symptoms that had gradually worsened now made sense; the fear—malignancy.

But not all brain tumors are malignant, as I well knew, for when I was five years old my grandfather had been operated on for brain tumors. Grandpa too had terrible symptoms—excruciating headaches, dizziness, and finally seizures. Grandma was alone with him the night he had his most acute attack before his disease was finally diagnosed correctly. She took him to another doctor, who, with the instinct of all fine diagnosticians, and without any test results to go by, said, "I think Art has a brain tumor. Take him to the hospital." He was right. Grandpa didn't die that night, as grandma had been sure he would, but lived to undergo successful brain surgery, only to die from pneumonia while in the hospital. No, a brain tumor need not be malignant to kill.

Stan, however, was more fortunate than my grandfather. Neurophysiologists know much more about the brain today than they did thirty years ago, and so Stan's doctors operated and eventually released him from the hospital a well man. Grateful, he began to live again, which meant finding a job and moving—from Manhattan to Michigan, the kind of move that would take any family some adjustment.

Shortly after he arrived, I met him at our local needlepoint store, as unlikely a place to meet a man as I could imagine. (I know several men who needlepoint, but I've never seen any male in that particular store, not in seven years.) Stan lived near the store and decided to inspect it for his wife, who was the needlepointer in the family. He still bore the scars of his surgery; his hair was only beginning to grow back and the jagged incision on his scalp and forehead was clearly visible. Involuntarily, I shuddered when I looked at it, seeing my grandpa's face and wondering whether his incision had looked like Stan's. I never knew because the hospital wouldn't let children visit patients.

As I thought about grandpa, I continued to ask Stan questions, the ordinary questions someone asks a newcomer: Were they all moved in? How did they like their new house? New job? Had they found a church yet? If not, why not try ours? I also asked some not-so-ordinary questions: How are you feeling? What do the doctors say? How long were you ill before you learned about your problem? We'd love to have you over for supper sometime soon—we'll call you.

But we never did.

Stan believed that his physical troubles were over. Hadn't his doctors said so? Didn't they know more now than they had when my grandfather had surgery? Didn't they?

I saw Stan again a few months later at a convention, looking tired and hot at the end of the day—but it *was* hot in Southern California, so I thought nothing of it. "We've got to get together soon," I said. "It's ridiculous to come all the way out here when we live just a few miles from each other." "You're right," he said. "Let's plan to have dinner." We became separated in the crowd and didn't see each other again. I returned home, intending to invite him to dinner—but the time never came.

Some things should never be put off, and this was one, as I discovered too late. A few months later I learned that Stan was back in the hospital. The doctors weren't as wise as they had bragged, for Stan's tumors had returned, still benign, but what difference did it make? "We can't understand it," they told him. He faced another surgery, and then another, and then . . . The tumors would not go away.

Just as I never saw my grandfather again, I never saw Stan again. He couldn't take any more surgery. Why did Stan's life fall apart and that of his wife and daughter? Did their faith falter, as mine would, as, if we are honest, most of ours would? Why should such brutality happen to so gentle a person? Where is the blessing to be found?

Life swings back and forth precariously, and death, many kinds of death, threaten to leap on the swing with us—the playground bully who delights in cursing and tormenting us just as we swing our highest and laugh our most delighted.

Where is the hero who can put the bully in his place?

Enter the Hero

"*Did you ever* see such a crowd, Sarah? This Rebbe must be some wise man."

"Wise guy, you mean. That's what our leaders say. They won't like this at all—and right before Passover. You know how nervous the Romans get during any of our big feasts. How are your preparations coming?"

"Fine, fine. You know I'm never behind in my work. But if you think this Rebbe is such a wise guy, what are you doing here with the rest of us?"

"Did I say I believed those bloodsuckers? Anyway, who isn't here today? The Reb might perform a miracle the way I've heard he's done other places. Or he might put those pompous priests in their place. He's done it before, or so they say. No one can figure out what the man means half the time—loves the riddles, just like all wise men, or guys, whichever you prefer."

"Hmph. Riddles. That's nothing to what I heard about the stories he tells—makes everyone angry, like the time he told the one about the stupid man who got himself stripped, robbed, and near beaten to death traveling by himself on the road to Jericho."

"Jericho? What a fool. No one travels that road alone."

"So what? That didn't stop the Rebbe from making it part of the tale, though that wasn't the worst of it. He made the hero a Samaritan, may the Master of the Universe grant that such a one never receive eternal life. Of course, he also shamed the priests and Levites too. Not that they don't deserve it, I'll admit—but to contrast them with an infidel because he stopped to help when no one else would. Why *would* a priest do such a thing? The man might have been dead or, worse, a Gentile. Who could tell when he had no clothes and couldn't speak? But if he had been a Jew—imagine how he would have felt, being helped by a cursed one. That's the kind of ridiculous tale the Rebbe gives the crowds."

"But who would believe such a story? No good Jew would let a Samaritan touch him, unless he couldn't prevent it. Given a choice, I'd rather die than accept help from one of those. No wonder the Rebbe makes people angry—"

"Sh! I think I see some commotion, but isn't it hard to tell through all the palm branches? Quite a greeting for someone who stirs things up, isn't it?"

"A donkey—he's riding a donkey, just like one of us. Catch Annas or Caiphas riding into town on a jackass. Not likely. Well, there he goes. I guess he doesn't plan to stop after all." The woman turned away.

"Where are you going, Sarah?"

"You might not be behind, but I am. The show's over."

The two women separated, dropping their branches in the dust, immediately forgetting the momentary excitement. Peter and John, the Rebbe's close friends, watched the women and the rest of the crowd leave.

"Why did they come, do you suppose?" Peter asked.

"Excitement. Or following their neighbors. Who knows? But the Rebbe didn't seem to pay much attention to the adulation from the crowd. Yet I've never seen the people so eager to greet him. And it *was* exciting while it lasted, though I wish he hadn't insisted on coming here. Did you notice the priest in the back of the crowd?"

"Yes, and I'm certain the Master did, as well, because he shuddered as we rode by him. Something's bothering the Master, though he ignores my questions when I ask him about it."

"Peter, I've noticed the same thing. He's preoccupied, almost withdrawn. He spends more time than ever in prayer, and he's eaten little in the last few days. Well, soon it'll be Passover. We'd better ask the Rebbe what his plans are."

As the men continued to talk, they walked in the direction the Master and the donkey had gone, soon reaching him.

"The crowds have left, Master," Peter told him.

"Yes, I knew they'd leave soon, and yet it was time for the greeting. The next time the crowd will sound a different word. But will I be prepared? Is there time?"

"Master, of course there is. The Passover's a few days off yet. Tell us where we will remember the Covenant, and we will take care of everything."

"Yes, Peter, the Passover. I have not forgotten. An innkeeper has offered his upper room for our meal; no one else will want such a small, smelly spot. Go and see that at least he cleans it properly."

"Yes, Master. I'll take care of everything," and Peter left.

The night of the Passover, Peter studied the room with satisfaction. The Master would be pleased with the meal—if only he would leave his mood behind. Peter heard the disciples coming up the stairs and turned to greet them, waiting for the Master to indicate where each one should sit, though he knew that he and John would be closest to him. The Master did not disappoint him when he pointed Peter to his seat.

Halfway through the meal Peter was pleased with the way things were going, only regretting that he and John had argued about which of them would be first in the kingdom. So foolish, so prideful, as they saw when the Master faced them. Peter again chided himself on his hasty, haughty disposition. Would he never learn? Peter shook his head and listened to the Rebbe.

What was the Master saying? Something about a broken body and betrayal? So he *was* worried about the priests. Now where was Judas going? Probably to relieve himself. He always drinks too much, thought Peter with disgust. Why the Master ever chose him—the man had no self-control—Peter could not understand. He tried to hide a yawn and began to think of his bed.

"I am going to Gethsemane to pray this night, and I want my disciples with me," the Master said, turning to Peter just as Peter began another, broader yawn.

"But Master, why tonight? It's late and we're tired."

"You will know soon why I must pray tonight. Now, let us leave—and don't argue."

Peter tried to hide his disappointment as he and the others rose reluctantly to follow Jesus. The Master seemed to need less and less sleep, but that didn't hold true for the rest of them. As they left the inn, Jesus turned to Peter and said, "I fear for you. This night you will learn a bitter truth about yourself—your cowardice and your disloyalty—but face it and find forgiveness as a gift of the kingdom."

"Master, I don't understand you. If you're in danger, don't taunt me with such vague words. You know I'll never desert you."

"Do I, Peter? Do I? You do not understand how much you love your life—three times before the cock crows you will show that love to yourself. But remember the forgiveness. Now let us go quickly, for much has yet to happen this night."

Although later Peter tried to remember each detail of what happened, he could never recall much. The prayers of the Master, his anger at finding his disciples asleep, the priests and Judas greeting the Master, then the accusations and denials—all as the Master had warned. But the tears, those Peter could still taste. He and the others alternated between hope that the authorities would release their Lord and anguish that they would not. Helpless, they watched him beaten, and horrified, they heard the crowd call for Barabbas.

"How dare they?" Peter asked John. "Can these be the same people who shouted praises only a short time ago?"

"Peter, these are the same. See over there the old women we noticed last week, still jabbering, only look at the difference in their faces. I fear for the Master now. You know how Pilate cringes before an angry crowd of us Jews; almost, I believe, he fears us more than he fears his emperor. Here he comes."

"You stay if you want to. I'm going back to the inn. Meet me there later and tell me what he says."

*   *   *

Heroes aren't supposed to die, even if they suffer, and no one likes an unhappy ending—not Peter, not any of us. We want our stories and our heroes to brave danger and trample the wicked, not bow meekly under the lash. But even here—or we might say *especially* here—God chooses the victim, not the vindicator, the vanquished, not the vanquishing. Then and only then does the blessing come. The foolish man traveling alone on the road to Jericho, where he knows he should not be, but finally unable to resist the grace that was the result of his nakedness, his wounds, and his stupidity—Jesus becomes this man, and so must we, victims all, clothed in the cloak of God's grace and blessing, the garment of the Sovereign.

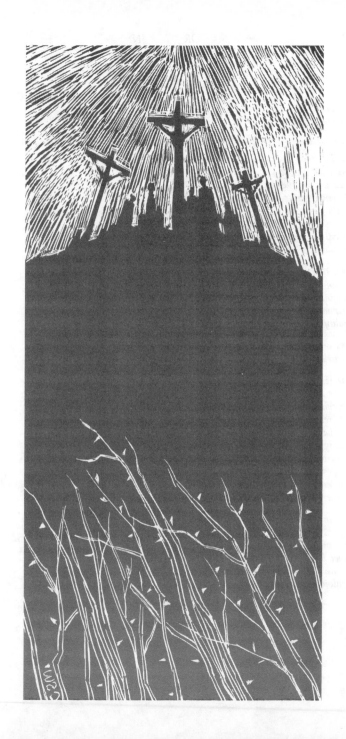

*Broadmoor Books are different.
They are for the discriminating
Christian reader who admires fine
writing and desires to be challenged
by fresh, unconventional, and even
unsettling expressions of historical
orthodoxy.*

*Each book in this series has been
chosen for its literary merit and
imaginative appeal. Every effort has
been made to achieve a high level of
quality in design and production.*

*Broadmoor Books aspire to be the
Christian classics of the future.*

*The text of Backdoor Blessings is
set in 10/14 Palatino. Designed by
Hermann Zapf in 1948, Palatino is a
rich reinterpretation of oldstyle type
and has a subtly calligraphic feel.
The type was set on a Mergenthaler
Linotron 202/N by the Photo-
composition Department of
Zondervan Publishing House; Judy
Schafer, compositor.*

*The interior was designed by Louise
Bauer. The illustrations were drawn
by Corey Scott Wilkinson, and the
cover is by Koechel-Peterson Design.
Printed by Patterson Printing of
Benton Harbor, Michigan.*